The Lunar Mansions Guide
Rediscovering the Western Lunar Zodiac

The Lunar Mansions Guide
Rediscovering the Western Lunar Zodiac

Oscar Hofman

THE WESSEX ASTROLOGER

Published in 2022 by
The Wessex Astrologer Ltd
PO Box 9307
Swanage
BH19 9BF

For a full list of our titles go to www.wessexastrologer.com

© Oscar Hofman 2022
Oscar Hofman asserts his moral right to be recognised as
the author of this work

ISBN 9781910531686

Cover design by Andy Jay

A catalogue record for this book is available at The British Library

No part of this book may be reproduced or used in any form or by any
means without the written permission of the publisher.
A reviewer may quote brief passages.

Table of Contents

Preface		vii
Part 1	The Cosmological Backgrounds	1
Part 2	The 28 Lunar Mansions – Their essences, myths, effects and natures	11
	1. Al Sharatain	17
	2. Al Butain	22
	3. Al Thurayya	27
	4. Al Dabaran	33
	5. Al Haqa	38
	6. Al Hana	43
	7. Al Dhira	49
	8. Al Natrah	54
	9. Al Tarf	59
	10. Al Jabbah	64
	11. Al Zubrah	69
	12. Al Sarfah	75
	13. Al Awwa	80
	14. Al Simak	84
	15. Al Ghafr	90
	16. Al Zubana	95
	17. Al Iklil	100
	18. Al Qalb	105

19. Al Shaulah	110
20. Al Na'am	115
21. Al Baldah	120
22. Al Sa'd al Dhabhi	125
23. Al Sa'd Bula	131
24. Al Sa'd al Suud	137
25. Al Sa'd – Akhbiya	142
26. Al Fargh al–Awwal	146
27. Al Fargh al Thani	152
28. Al Batn al Hut	157
Appendix A Comparing Arabian and Vedic mansions, medical correspondences	163
Appendix B The all-important precession	166
Appendix C The planetary parts, essential energies	175
Appendix D An explanation of dignities and receptions	177
Epilogue	185
Bibliography	186
About the Author	188

Preface

Since 1980 traditional astrology has been growing and growing; old knowledge that had seemed lost forever has been retrieved, and at the time of writing (in 2021) traditional astrology has found its place in the astrological world. This development was quite unexpected in 1980 and is closely connected to an important astrological phenomenon, the cycle of the Great Conjunctions of Saturn and Jupiter (GCs). The GCs occur in signs of one element for about 200 years before moving into the next element. This is always mirrored in our sub-lunar world by profound social, cultural, political and technological changes. It was exactly this process that started in 1980 when the GCs moved into the Air element after 200 years of being in Earth.

Part of this transition into the Air element is a stream of new knowledge, and in the astrological world this has manifested in the recovery of the treasures of an astrological tradition of more than twenty centuries. The English theosophical astrologers who regenerated our celestial art at the end of the 19th century got rid of almost all the methods which had previously been used by astrologers and created their own form of astrology. This was the root of what is known now as 'modern astrology'. Traditional astrology goes back to how astrology was before this theosophical revolution. As from 2020 the transition process of the Grand Conjunctions to Air will be finalised (there was as usual an intermediary Earth phase from 2000 to 2020) and it can expected that the new 'old' knowledge of traditional astrology will be brought to its full flowering.

The Lunar Mansions Guide

This guide on the lunar mansions is part of this development. It aims at retrieving and regenerating an important old method which, in Western astrology at least, has unfortunately become quite obsolete. In my book *Fixed Stars in the Chart – Constellations, Lunar Mansions and Mythology* (The Wessex Astrologer 2019) I devoted a chapter to the lunar mansions as they are so strongly connected to the fixed stars. This was partly based on information from Vedic astrology, which has always honoured the mansions; the information was translated directly into Western terms without applying any Vedic techniques.

This worked well enough. Nevertheless, it was not totally satisfactory as there are also the Arabian mansions, fully part of our own Western tradition. The problem is that what can be found in the texts about the Arabian mansions seems to be quite corrupted, incomplete and often rather confusing. But on the basis of further investigations and especially practical application a method could be developed to make a practical effective use of the Arabian mansion system possible again in natal, electional and predictive astrology. It was based on a very critical evaluation of old texts and on the knowledge of the fixed stars, their natures and especially their mythological stories. This method is presented in this guide, which can thus be seen as a companion to the book on the fixed stars.

Many complex problems had to be solved, a process which is instructive in itself as it goes back to the roots of astrology. There is a lot to learn here not only practically but also theoretically and cosmologically. The precession is one of the central themes in this whole process, as the lunar mansions are found in the sphere of the fixed stars which is exactly the sphere that makes the precessional movement within the sphere of the 'Zodiacal Towers', that is, the signs. Understanding the precession clearly is understanding the lunar mansions clearly. The result is a practical guide enabling you to make effective use of the lost Arabian mansions and to enrich your chart delineations considerably with the information they have to offer.

In this way astrology will return more and more to the sacred science it once was, showing how intimately connected our every breath is to the divine source through the intermediary of the signs, the mansions and the planets.

TO THE GLORY OF GOD!

July 2021 Gorinchem, The Low Lands,
next door to The Red Lyon.

Part 1

The Cosmological background

In order to thoroughly understand the lunar mansions, we start where it all begins, with the signs of zodiac. The tropical zodiac is of fundamental importance in astrology and its structure is directly derived from the solar cycle. This is most appropriate as the Sun is the visible symbol of God's activity in the cosmos and the first 'product' of this creative activity is the zodiacal circle. It should be clearly understood that the zodiac was not discovered by the keen observations of some smart Babylonian proto-scientists in days of yore. This would be an unjustifiable projection of our materialistic and scientific prejudices on the past. The zodiac is on the contrary a cosmological-metaphysical idea revealed, protected and passed on by tradition and passing on is exactly what the word tradition means.

The Jewish story is that our celestial art was taught by Adam to his son Seth in the Garden of Eden. This means symbolically that astrology was *given* to mankind (revealed), not invented or developed by long observation. Just think of a constellation like Corvus, the Crow - you would have to smoke a lot of strange stuff to see a crow in the Crow. Nevertheless, its main Crow star, Algorab, has exactly the effects you could expect on the basis of the myth connected to the Crow. So the truth is out there, but observation alone could not possibly access this truth. The same argument holds true for the other parts of the astrological system. Our celestial art was revealed, but how exactly this was done I leave to your imagination.

The cosmology shows that the only zodiac at the root of astrology is the tropical zodiac; every variation, like the sidereal zodiac used in Hindu astrology for example, is derived from it.

So it all starts with the Sun and its cyclical movement. In this movement there are four important points, the equinoxes and the solstices, which mark the space in the centre of the cosmos where we live on earth. There can be no doubt about these points; they are crystal-clear astronomical facts and they indicate the four cardinal signs, out of which the whole zodiac springs forth. Of course, the vernal equinox, 0° Aries, is the most prominent among these four points as it is the starting-point of the zodiac, marking the birth of a new year regardless of your geographical position on earth.

It is no coincidence that the zodiacal girdle contains exactly 12 signs. Based on number symbolism, 12 is 3 x 4. 4 is the number of material manifestation, which is why we have four elements. The number 3 refers to the spirit, to the creative activity, which comes down, works out on earth and returns to its source. These three modes are expressed in the zodiac as the moveable (cardinal), fixed and double-bodied (mutable) signs. As multiplication refers to potential, 3 x 4 gives us all the creative possibilities; the zodiac contains the total potential of creation, and the four elements can be seen in it in their three phases of manifestation. As a process of which our lives are a part, it depicts the returning of the creative impulse through matter to its divine source.

Also the nature of the moveable (cardinal) signs is given by the solar cycle; the equinoxes in Aries and Libra can be associated with heat, as these are active phases. The solstices, to the contrary, are extreme phases during which developments come to a standstill and turn around. Therefore the solstice signs Capricorn and Cancer are cold, although fertile Cancer is moist and Capricorn is dry. Both points are connected with a feast of Saint John. Cancer at the start of summer is associated with the feast of Saint John the Baptist - things may seem nice now but the cycle has turned around and it is gradually going to get darker and colder, it is time to do penance. Capricorn is the time of Saint John the Evangelist, announcing the birth of the Saviour - things may seem dark now but the light will soon be born again, another turning of the cycle at an extreme point.

The zodiac is a blueprint, directly related to the solar cycle, but in a way it is still quite abstract. This is indicated by the fact that the zodiac is invisible; the signs cannot be seen and the fact that we have 12 parts of exactly 30°, with totally clear boundaries, is like an ideal construct. It is a sound metaphysical principle that something that cannot be seen is 'higher', closer to the source than something that can be seen. The zodiac shows all the potential that will manifest in creation, so it is most appropriate that it is the royal path of the Sun, the symbol of the divine source, the symbol of God. There is nothing above or behind the zodiac except God, no other structures that tell us anything about our lives as human beings on this earth; there is only the divine origin, only the Ain Soph, the limitless light as described by the Kabbalah.

To manifest, however, the Sun (the Greater Luminary) must be in a relationship with the Moon (the Lesser Luminary), guiding the solar impulses to earth. The Moon is in that sense a symbol for the totality of earthly life. Its constantly changing shape clearly indicates this role reflecting the ever-changing forms of life on earth.

So the Moon is a much more earthy planet than the Sun, more connected with our daily lives as the Lesser Luminary and therefore we may expect that the path of the Moon, the lunar mansions or the lunar zodiac, will be less abstract and perfect than the signs, the solar mansions of the zodiac.

This is shown by the fact that the lunar mansions are very much connected to the stars and the constellations they mark, and the stars are visible, which is a sign they are lower in the creative hierarchy. The lunar mansions are always presented as the path of the Moon, its daily progress *against the background* of the fixed stars, and the sphere of the fixed stars is indeed found *below* the invisible solar energy girdle of the zodiacal signs.

This is reflected by the movement of the Moon, which has a cycle of 27.3 days (which can be rounded up to 28 or down to 27). In the Vedic system of the lunar mansions we have 27 mansions in the basic pattern, whereas in the Arabian system we have the circle divided into 28 parts. So the lunar mansion gives in a very basic way the part of the sky through which the Moon is moving *today*. This number, 28, is (almost) an astronomical fact and it is highly symbolic. It consists of the numbers 1 to 7 all added up. Adding up points symbolically creates something more concrete in the physical life. This can also be seen as 3 + 4, adding up to 7 – the number of classical planets which realise the potential of the 12-fold zodiac on earth.

In that sense it is still a kind of zodiac, a systemized girdle of energies giving the Moon placed in it a certain character. We could say there are 28 ways the Moon can be coloured by the mansions. As a mansion is connected to the stars, it is always associated with a mythical story, and here we see the first practical guideline for delineation. This is a big, big difference from placement in signs - a position in a sign *never ever* gives you a connection with a myth!

It is also helpful in this context to understand what the sidereal zodiac is exactly. It is used in Vedic astrology but it is essentially the same zodiac as the tropical zodiac. It also consists of twelve invisible equal parts of 30° length with absolutely clear boundaries between the signs, bearing the same names as the tropical signs. The only difference is that the starting-point in the sidereal zodiac - 0° Aries - is not the vernal equinox point. The beginning of Aries is on the contrary fixed by connecting it to a star (sider = star), in most cases this is the point opposing Spica, so the sidereal zodiac moves *through* the tropical zodiac at a precessional speed of one degree every 72 years. We will come back to this below as this is relevant for the lunar mansions, which like the sidereal zodiac, are sidereal, connected to the stars.

The movement of the zodiac by precession in Vedic/Hindu astrology has to do with a deep cultural difference between the polytheistic Indian

East and the monotheistic West. The Hindu spirit tends "to dissolve things in the consent of the Infinite", as the metaphysician Titus Burkhardt says, to make the connection to God. The monotheistic spirit is less fluid and tends to deduce things from the viewpoint of absolute divine unity. So these two choices mirror different ways of using astrology as a sacred science, of which the central issue is how to connect to God. It should be understood that Hinduism, despite its apparent polytheism, also contains this idea of the unity of the divine.

The 28-fold lunar zodiac can also be projected onto the 12-fold solar zodiac, starting at 0°Aries; we can call this the 'archetypical order'. It then indicates 28 creative steps from the first impulse to complete realisation. In this way, being closer to our daily lives in material reality than the abstract solar zodiac, it shows how the potentials in the solar zodiac are more tangibly realised. Every mansion carries the meaning of one of these 28 steps. This 'step' nature of the mansions will be mentioned in Part 2 where all 28 mansions will be described. The mansions work out the solar potential.

The starting-point

This brings us to the hottest theoretical question which has caused lots of confusion, so fasten your seat-belts. In fact, this shows the reason the lunar mansions have become obsolete in Western astrology. This question is: where does the lunar zodiac, the cycle of the lunar mansions start? At which point in the zodiac do we find the first mansion of the Ram's Horn, Al Sharatain? The best way to discuss this complicated matter is to consider four possibilities and then evaluate them to pick the best one. These are the four options.

Option A - Start at 0° Aries tropical, this is the archetypical option.

Option B – Start at the point most often used in the Hindu system at the degree opposing Spica, now at 24° Aries tropical - this is the Vedic option.

Option C – Start at the first star in the first mansion - Mesarthim - now at 3°11 Taurus tropical. This is the precessed option.

Option D - Also start at the first star in the first mansion, Mesarthim at 3°11 Taurus, but in this option there are varying lengths of the mansions, the boundaries determined by bright fixed stars. This is the constellational option. In fact D is the same as C regarding the starting-point but it uses another method to fix the boundaries of the mansions.

Options A, B and C all use mansions of equal length of 12°51'36", so one mansion is exactly 1/28 of the circle.

Below the options will be discussed, their pros and cons weighed, after which a choice will be made.

Option A - The Archetypical Option
At first glance this is the best option by far. The point where the first mansion of the Ram's Horn starts is the same as the vernal equinox point; everything is as crisp and clear as you could wish and this is the option many authors prefer. BUT, this would mean that because of the precession, the Mansion of the Ram's Horn would no longer contain the fixed stars that are said to mark and characterize that mansion. For a lunar system explicitly connected to the sphere of the visible fixed stars this is too weird, so we cannot possibly accept this. The stars are precessed so the mansions – the 'star houses' - have to be precessed too. The idea of the mansion cycle and the zodiac starting both at the same point is of theoretical importance for understanding the nature of the mansions, but for operational purposes (practical delineation), it cannot be used.

Another characteristic of the mansions system confirms this. In the whole series of 28 mansions several constellations appear more than once;

Leo, for example, rules no less than four mansions. Being big seems to be quite appropriate for Leo, but it shows that the mansion system follows the reality of the fixed stars and constellations closely. The constellation of Leo is right on the zodiac and it is one of the longer constellations. Four Leo mansions cover almost 50 degrees, so it is very clear that the mansions are not modelled on the basis of the zodiac, but on the constellational level of the stars, and the stars are precessed.

Interestingly enough, this brings us to what caused the confusion in the old texts. Around 400 BC the constellational sphere of the fixed stars and the tropical zodiac itself coincided. So the first point of the Aries constellation (the star Mesarthim) was close to 0° Aries tropical. At that point the two spheres seemed to be strongly connected or even the same, but the constellations are slowly precessing away from the signs they are related to and we have to take this into account.

Option B - The Vedic Option

In Vedic astrology, just like in Option A, the first Aries mansion starts at the same point as the sidereal zodiac. The problem with this is that the Vedic zodiac is sidereal, so the starting-point of the mansion cycle and the Aries sign has to be fixed by a star position. In Vedic astrology this is usually the degree opposing Spica, but there are many other options and there is a lot of discussion about the correct choice.

Spica is the Wheat-ear in Virgo, a symbol of purification of the material level so that it can receive the spiritual energy; it is in fact the material returning itself to the spirit. The Wheat-Ear is the concentration point where the harvest of material experiences is gathered and processed. The point opposing Spica would be the reverse, the spiritual coming down into matter which would be a good description of Aries, so this is probably the reason Spica was chosen to mark the starting-point. This fixed 0° Aries sidereal and the beginning of the first lunar mansion in Vedic astrology is near the star Revati or zèta Piscium at about 24° Aries tropical.

The problem is that this means the starting-point of the sidereal zodiac is in the middle of the constellation of Pisces, so not really close to the first star of the Aries constellation at all - there is a 7-degree distance. So in Vedic astrology the starting-point is not directly indicated by a bright or first star of a constellation, despite the fact that the lunar mansions are said to give the movement of the Moon against the background of the fixed stars. The basic problem is that the constellations have blurred boundaries, as is their nature, so it is not easy to find the exact place where Pisces ends and Aries begins. That is why Vedic/sidereal astrologers disagree about the choice of the starting-point. In fact they are looking for something that is not clearly indicated. Nevertheless, this is not a bad choice.

Another point of view would be that every choice gives you a system of a different nature. So if you choose to start it all at the point opposing Spica or Chitra as the Hindus do, you have a system of an 'opposite-Spica' nature. It would be characterized by this Virgo purifying tendency, whereas starting with the first star of Aries would give you a system more characterized by the Aries impulse to get involved in the world, and after this finally sacrifice the worldly ego to return to the divine. This does seem to mirror the cultural differences between the active materialistic West and more contemplative India.

Option C - *The Precessed Option*

Looking for a suitable starting-point we could say that it must be found somewhere between the last star of Pisces and the first star of Aries. Somewhere in this region there is a transition to the Aries constellational zone. The problem is there is only empty space, so where is it? The point between the last Pisces star Alresha and the first Aries star seems to be a bit too easy as a choice. Would it be better to choose the very first star in Aries, Mesarthim, currently at 3.11 Taurus tropical? It is one of the stars ruling the first Mansion, Al Sharatain, and it is right at the beginning of Aries. Imagine you are travelling from the constellation Pisces following the solar

The Cosmological background

royal path of the zodiac, you would after some time of walking through an empty landscape suddenly see the Horn of Mesarthim appearing on the other side of a hill as a sign you had entered a new region.

So this is the best choice, as it keeps this strong connection with the constellations, it respects the precession and it is very logical to start a cycle beginning with the Ram's Mansion with the first star in the Ram. It is true that in this way a kind of 'constellational cusp' is created and this idea may seem a bit dubious. Nevertheless, the traditional pictures of the constellations show that Aries, the first zodiacal constellation, has no overlap with Pisces, so there is no blurring there. This is a special case justifying the fixation of a starting-point. After all, Aries is the most special sign, the *primus inter pares,* as it all starts at this point, it symbolises in this way all that will be there.

It is the famous or maybe notorious author of the *Three Books of Occult Philosophy* (February 1531), Henry Cornelius Agrippa of Nettesheim, who drives the point home very clearly: "the lunar mansions are fixed in the eighth sphere", that is the sphere of the fixed stars! He also says that the first mansion which he calls Alnath, the Horns of Aries, has its beginning from the head of Aries *in the eighth sphere.* So he is talking about the constellations there (the eighth sphere), **not** about the signs which are found in the ninth sphere. Thinking clearly, as he often does, Agrippa is using his brain here rather than indiscriminately copying old texts.

Option D - *The Constellational Option*

In some texts the mansions are given very different lengths, the idea being that a mansion starts at the exact position of an acceptable bright star and continues to the next star marking the start of the next mansion. This is ugly and unacceptable, as it ignores the fact that the Moon gives us a rhythm of 27/28 days allowing for a more rigid systematization, a division of the circle by 28 (or 27 as in India). It takes the idea of connecting the mansions to the visible stars too far, it is too literal. Moreover, this would lead to a multiplication of problems by 28, as which stars should be counted exactly as marking the mansion boundaries? This option can be disregarded, and it is only mentioned because some authors present this as the lunar mansion system, which could be quite confusing.

Precession

We have made our choice; this selection process was shared because there is so much to learn here about the principles of astrology. More on the precession, its mysterious nature and the untenable and illogical idea of the Age of Aquarius can be found in Appendix B.

Part 2

The 28 mansions – their effects, natures and myths

The special function of the Moon is clear in the model of the astrological spheres - which is absolutely necessary for a good understanding of astrology (also see Appendix B on the precession). The highest sphere is the zodiac, below it is the sphere of the fixed stars and the lunar mansions, then the seven planet spheres in descending order; all these influences descend on earth/the human being at the centre of the whole cosmos. In this path of the creative impulse coming down, the Moon is the last 'station' before it reaches the earth.

The Traditional Model of the Spheres

This is why it is always said that the Moon collects the energies from the higher spheres and through the Moon they reach the earth (reflected for example also in the role of the Moon as the co-significator of the querent in horary astrology). So the Moon is very important; it gives us the general 'ambience' and the mansion where the Moon falls is a good description of this ambience. This shows us how the Mansions can be used in astrological practice. Obviously then, they will be useful as one of several factors in a complete election, but also to make quick elections for daily use. Moreover, in natal astrology the mythological story, the themes and keywords connected to the mansion will play an important role as the core myth in the life. Also in predictive astrology the movement of the secondary progressed Moon through the mansions is an important factor.

As the secondary progressed Moon's speed is about one degree a month, it will be in a mansion for about a year. So it can be used as *one* of the predictive factors to get a picture of what will be happening in the life in a year's prognosis. It will often be the case that the secondary progressed Moon will enter a new mansion and this offers the opportunity to describe this movement for your client as a process of development. As prediction is always based on astrological factors *changing* their conditions, this may give us important clues about what is to be expected. This also depends on the condition of the mansion the Moon is moving through in the natal chart, as will be explained in the delineation scheme below.

In connection with elective use it is necessary to say something about elections for magical operations, often mentioned in the old texts. In every balanced traditional society based on sound spiritual principles, magic is seen as an illegal and even dangerous activity. Magic is a real science, a structured body of knowledge like modern science, only rather than working with material forces it works with subtle or psychic forces in the astral world. The astral world contains the subtle forms which can manifest on the material plane. So by manipulating the astral energies by symbols, magic can have very real effects both psychologically and materially.

The 28 mansions – their effects, natures and myths

The astral plane is, however, also the home of the Faeries, or in Islamic terms the Jinn, and all kinds of astral entities who are not necessarily always malefic, but contacts with them should be strictly avoided. The idea of the powerful mage using astral energies and entities is very misleading. Magic is always a contract with Mephisto: "Dear soul, I will give you some powers you will like a lot, but in exchange I will take a little bit of you, and next time another little bit. Sign here with your blood please." Part of the demonic trick is that the mage thinks he is in control but in fact he is controlled. Direct contact with the astral dimensions is psychologically or even physically disturbing; I have seen too many tragic examples.

It should also be avoided for reasons of psychological hygiene. The most tragic case is the 'white' magus, who wants to use his powers to do good. Using astral energies in this way always harms and un-balances the operator and his 'client'. Even talismans made for healing purposes are potentially dangerous, as things will get out of hand easily and backfire on the magus or the client. A short look around the New Age bookshop near you will be enough to conclude that psychological hygiene is not a thing people in these times are very much concerned about. What was said about magic also applies to other ways to force an entry into the astral dimension, like spiritualism, contacting elemental spirits and taking psychedelic drugs like LSD.

It is an understatement to say that not all magical elections mentioned in connection with the mansions seem to be of a beneficial nature. Magic is dangerous for the operator, his environment and for society in general. It is only the demons that laugh in the end. Naivety, hubris, ambition, curiosity or a combination of them is fatal here. The reason that the lunar mansions are often mentioned in connection with magical elections is that they give us the state of the Moon, which is a symbol of the astral-psychological ambience. A cursory glance at hospital statistics is enough to see the effect of the Full Moon on the human astral-psychological condition for example.

This however far exceeds the individual case; it concerns the collective and the whole 'astral-psychic' atmosphere.

Each of the 28 Mansions will be described as follows:

1. The traditional Arabic name will be given and if relevant explained.
2. Its mythological story will be told.
3. The descriptive stars will be given and the planets associated with them.
4. Tangible effects and keywords will be given.
5. The symbolic image connected to the mansion will be described.
6. The associated Arabic letter and its symbolism will be explained.

   Arabic, like Sanskrit, Hebrew and Latin, is a sacred language. The 28 letters of the Arabic alphabet are seen as creative sounds; the world is created by speaking, as you can also read in the first book of the Bible and in the famous beginning of the Gospel of Saint John. This is also the reason why prayer and spells are effective.

7. The step in the creative process that the mansion represents will be given.

   As explained above, the 28 mansions symbolise the complete creation process, every mansion being a step in this process. This is mentioned *only* to be complete; the direct practical application is not always as clear as you would wish, nevertheless the symbolism can be relevant so these creative steps are not left out.

8. The Vedic connections.

   In Hindu astrology the system of the mansions is different but certainly similar in structure. If the information about the parallel Vedic mansion is in some way clarifying it will be mentioned. See also Appendix C, in which both systems are compared.

The 28 mansions – their effects, natures and myths

9. An example chart is given, a natal chart, a prediction or an election illustrating the effect of the mansion.

The degrees given for the lunar mansions are those based on the position of Mesarthim, the first Aries star in 2000. To calculate the boundaries for the natal chart you are investigating, they should be adapted for precession, 1 degree in 72 years. So for 2020 16'40" (20/72 x 60') about a third of a degree should be added.

Note that the given boundaries of the mansions are rounded off because 360°/28 does not give you a nice number but 12,8571 which is 12°51'36". It would be very awkward to give boundaries in seconds of arc, all the more so as this is hardly ever relevant practically, so the consequence is a slight irregularity in length of the mansions, which again is hardly ever relevant. Moreover, it is very symbolic that the 'perfect' solar zodiac gives nice parts of exactly 30° (360:12) and the imperfect earthy Moon this impossible number, reflecting the nature of our sub-lunar world where exactness and perfection do not apply.

Delineation of the mansions

These steps should be taken to delineate a lunar mansion (all this information is found below in the discussion of all the 28 mansions).
1. Look up in which lunar mansion the Moon (only the Moon!) is placed natally.
2. Look up and explain the myth connected with the mansion as the core myth in the life.
3. Formulate the influence of the descriptive star(s) in the mansion.
4. Look up how strong the planets connected to the parts of the constellation in the mansion are placed natally (dignities, see Appendix D), the stronger they are, the more benefic the effect of the mansion (this is also important in prediction).

5. Check the indications and keywords the old texts give for the mansion.
6. Check the Vedic connection, to see if this has anything to add (see also *Fixed Stars in the Chart* Chapter 5).
7. Check the mansions through which the progressed Moon is moving and the mansion in the solar return the Moon is placed in, this information can serve as a predictive tool.

The natal lunar mansion will manifest in the context of the individual chart, but it can be seen as the central crystallisation point in the life; it will steer the whole life in a particular direction as a basic motive. However, it should be clearly understood that this is in no way limited to the psychological level. This basic motive will work out very tangibly but it is also strongly connected to the central myth. It is very important to see the Moon when delineating its mansion position not *as the Moon, not as one of the planets* but as the big hand in the lunar clock showing where in the mansion cycle development we are. Essentially the lunar mansions reflect the duality of our cosmos, founded as it is on polarity; there is not only a solar cycle – an idea – but also a lunar cycle – a manifestation.

The Lunar Mansions

First quarter of Seven Mansions

1. **Al Sharatain:** 3.11 Taurus - 16.02 Taurus
   Star: Sharatan/Mesarthim, the Ram's Horns
   Arabic letter: Alif
   Associated names: The Two Signals/The Warrior
   Associated planets and energies: Mars/Saturn – Dynamic power/fiery/impulsive/initiating energy

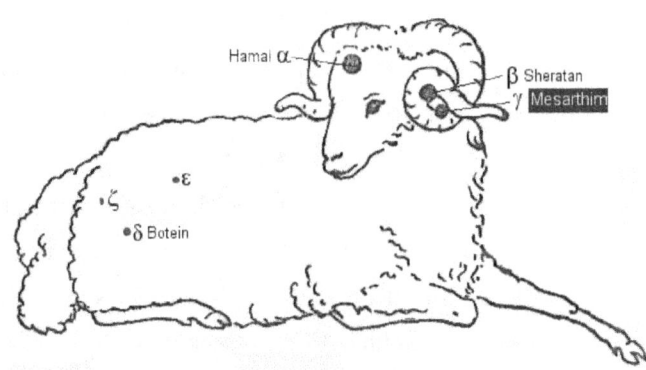

The name of this very first mansion of the Moon in Arabic means the Two Signals. This refers to the fact that the lunar zodiac starts at this point. As discussed above, the tropical degree occupied by the first star in the constellation of Aries, Mesarthim, is taken as the starting-point of the whole lunar mansions' cycle. This important point should be clearly marked, but these two signals are of course also connected to the two horns of Aries, an appropriate starting point for the fiery power to be used in a very concentrated, focused form. The splitting into two shows that we are entering the duality of creation, the separation between God and the world, at this point.

The star Sharatan, which gives this mansion its name, is one of the Horns of Aries, and Mesarthim itself, the first star is also on this horn. The myth of the Ram is the story of brother and sister Helle and Phryxos, who flew from their bad step-mother Ino who threatened to kill them. They escaped by flying over the sea on the back of the Ram but Helle, who looked down (focused her attention on the earthly world again), fell from its back and drowned. This water is still called the Sea of Helle, the Hellespont, which is also the border of Europe, the land of matter. Phryxos went on without his sister, reached safe grounds, sacrificed the Ram and gave the hide to King Aëtes, a son of Helios, the solar god. The Ram's hide is the Golden Fleece and is kept in a cave dedicated to Ares, the god of war.

People with the Moon in this mansion will relate to this story, which is full of symbolic meaning that has direct practical consequences. Phryxos and Helle as brother and sister are two parts of the soul. Helle, the female, more earth-bound part, falls down showing the fierceness of this mansion; it discards the more feminine side in order to get things done. Ino, the bad step-mother, is the symbol of matter, the rigid suffocating state from which they must escape. The sacrificed Ram's hide, the Golden Fleece, is hung on a tree so the Ram is also the Lamb, "That takes away the sins of this world". Looking for the Golden Fleece is seeking the divine, a spiritual goal; the sacrifice indicates the fiery Aries power should be used but after that we should honour God and let it go. The religious overtones are clear, just like the very fiery nature of this mansion (the Golden Fleece is kept in a cave dedicated to Ares).

The planetary energies are the malefics Mars and Saturn, combining hardness and fiery pushiness, so this mansion is not here to bring peace. It will forcefully initiate new things, break open stagnation and not be too concerned about resistance. The traditional image is that of a warrior holding a lance in his hand.

The 28 Mansions – Al Sharatain

 The associated Arabic Letter is the first letter, Alif. Its shape resembles the number one; it is said to belong to the Fire element and to symbolise the selfness of God as well as His unity, so it is all about the source from which the first impulse is given. It is also said to represent the whole alphabet, so it is all of creation summarized in a single letter.

The Ram's myth shows the essential task of man on earth, escaping from material bondage by avoiding the fall into the sea of desires (Helle's pont) and finally the sacrifice of the last wordly attachment (the Ram). The Ram is also the fierce impulse that would lead you back *into* the world again, which is why it has to be sacrificed. Christ, as the Lamb/Ram associated with this Aries mansion, is the Alpha (the Alef) and the Omega, which says more or less the same thing. The parallel Vedic mansion has the same meaning - it adds the preservation of the youthful energy as one of the keywords, which is a logical association. The name of the first step connected to the creative process represented by the mansions' cycle is 'The First Intellect,' or 'The Pen', that is going to write all the letters of creation. It mirrors the same idea of the first beginning.

This mansion is connected to fierceness, merciless battle, new beginnings and dedicated quests. In elections the Moon in this mansion is good for starting something brand new, to give a new fiery impulse; obviously this does not apply to love and marriage.

A good example of how this works out in a natal placement is the chart of the French president Emmanuel Macron, elected in 2017. Macron, with his brand-new party "En Marche!" which means something like "come on, let's get it done", won the presidency and a majority in parliament coming from nowhere, like a lightning bolt. He is trying to reform France, an old-fashioned half-socialist nation, into a modern liberal state. This would be a totally new phase, and he has met with a lot of resistance.

The Lunar Mansions Guide

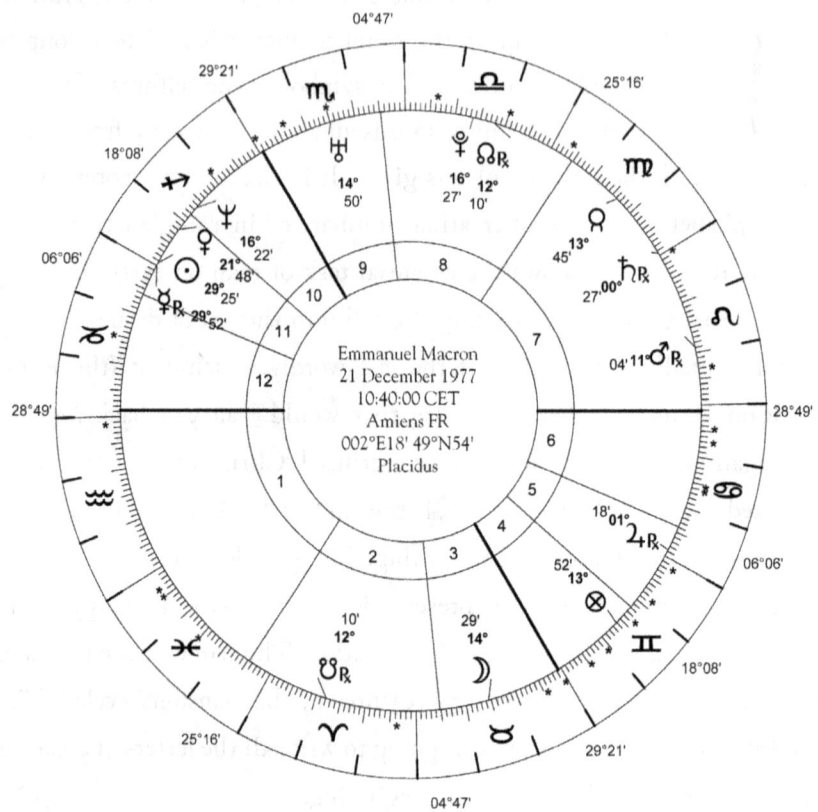

Of course, this is not the place for a complete delineation of his chart as we are focusing on the role of the lunar mansions. However, the natal mansion placement of the Moon giving us the core mythology and its more tangible implications always functions in the context of the rest of the chart, so a few more salient natal placements will be mentioned. One of them is Jupiter. Strong in its exaltation, the Great Benefic is the planet of politics, and the administrative elite making plans for the future. It is retrograde and if it goes back further, it will enter its detriment in Gemini, an enormous loss of power. So what the political planet wants is to move forward to avoid this fall into detriment: En Marche! This strengthens his need to move away from the past. Jupiter is Lord 11 of 'the fruits of your labour', so very much connected to public activities.

The other strong planet is the Moon. Also in its exaltation, the Moon is Lord 7. Lord 7 shows what is going on in relationships and Macron is married to a woman old enough to be his mother; the Moon is of course mothers. The Moon has lots of essential dignity so this lunar wife will be very good for him; it is a long, stable relationship. Saturn is the ruler of the first house, therefore Macron himself and his position in his life is also retrograde like Jupiter. This Saturn in the first degree of Virgo is about to lose a lot of dignity if it enters its detriment in Leo. Like Jupiter, it only wants to move forward and get away from the past.

The first degree of Virgo is also a very special degree in our times and is worth some extra attention. The most royal star of the royal stars, the Heart of the Lion, Regulus, 'that leads to the throne', has recently moved by precession over the Leo-Virgo boundary and it is now in the first degree of Virgo. So Saturn Lord 1/Macron himself will profit from the full royal powers dispensed by the Lion's Heart. This explains how he could appear like a lightning-bolt on the French political scene beating all his opponents and especially wiping out the complete political establishment. The author of the Harry Potter novels, J. K. Rowling, who also rose like lightning from a very low status as a single mother on social security to world fame, profited from the same movement - she has Mercury, the planet of writing, very strong in Virgo in the same degree. As you can see, you cannot do any proper astrology without fixed stars.

Al Sharatain of course describes Macron's political actions very well; this fiery start of a new cycle is strengthened and focused by the other positions in the chart that only want to move forward. The planetary rulers associated with this mansion, Saturn and Mars, tell us more about the way he will manifest the promise of the mansion. They are both placed in the angular seventh house so he will be able to get something done in the world, but it will hard-handed. Both malefics lack any essential dignity and therefore show their worst sides of aggressive power and harshness, which will meet a lot of resistance.

This is a first piece of evidence that the choice of the precessed option, taking Mesarthim as the starting-point of the cycle of the lunar mansions, is a very good idea. According to the archetypical option (starting the mansion cycle at 0° Aries tropical as explained above), the Moon would have been in the Al-Dabaran mansion, described by the powerful royal star Aldebaran. This fourth mansion also brings battles, but it lacks the strong notion of pioneering and of starting a new cycle so clearly seen in Macron's life. Moreover, if his Moon is seen as placed in the Al-Dabaran mansion it would be far away from the mansion's descriptive star found twenty-six degrees further at 10° Gemini. This enormous distance between the mansion and its descriptive star is unacceptable. It is remarkable that Macron rose to power in the Firdar (planet phase) of this strong exalted Moon, the general significator of the people.

---

2. **Al Butain:** 16.02 Taurus - 28.53 Taurus

   Star: Botein, the Ram's Belly/Tail

   Arabic letter: Haa

   Associated names: The Small Belly/The King

   Associated planets and energies: Mercury/Saturn – Fiery initiating energy (somewhat milder than the first mansion)/ possible reconciliation/giving form to the first impulse

The 28 Mansions – Al Butain

The second mansion in the lunar zodiac is also an Aries mansion, but as can be seen above the focus has shifted. Its name Al Butain means the Little Belly, to distinguish it from the 28th and final house, Al Batn-al Hut, which is the (big) Belly of the Fish (Hut). The focus has shifted from the power in the Horns to the hindpart of the Ram, an indication that a certain calming influence may be expected. The pure sharpness and violence of a totally new impulse, after its breaking through in Al Sharatain, is tempered a bit, so this is not as fierce as the first mansion. The ruling star is Botein and it is also sometimes said to be in the Tail of the Ram. It can be assumed that the difference between a horn and a tail needs no explanation.

Nevertheless, this is still part of Aries and its fiery nature certainly applies here too, as all the keywords of the Al Sharatain mansion, only in a milder or more tangible form. This illustrates that the mansions form a real interconnected series; it is the creative impulse moving through the complete cycle in consecutive steps. The meaning and effect of a mansion contributes to the meaning and effect of the next mansion; it is like life - the growing up and growing old of the creative impulse going through the 28 mansions. This is especially strong if the two mansions belong to the same constellation like here, where they can then be seen as two episodes of the same story.

So this mansion too has a connection to the myth of Phryxos and Helle. In a milder form it gives the same keywords, to which some extras have been added. In the Vedic system these two mansions are almost exactly the same as in our Arabic variety, belonging to the two parts of the Ram. Remarkably enough, the descriptive stars in the Vedic series are said to be three small stars in the 'belly' of Aries 'looking like a vagina', therefore this mansion is associated with sexuality and giving birth. It seems as if the Arabian 'belly' also refers to this.

This is more than logical, because the fires of Aries bursting forth in Al Sharatain, in the Horns, will connect more in this second milder Aries mansion. Also being in the body of the Ram, the free-burning impulse takes on a physical, sexual form which becomes fertile and bears fruit. The descriptive star is near the tail where the Aries constellation finishes, and birth is given.

The Arabic letter is Haa. It represents the number 5, referring to the original fifth element, Ether, from which the other four elements spring forth. It is said to be a symbol of orientation towards God (the Golden Fleece, to escape from material Ino).

This is the phase in which the totally pure fiery original impulse will become matter. It also indicates that this close to the starting point the warrior spirit is still very much present. The name of Phryxos' sister, Helle, seems to suggest a connection with Hellas or Greece, where the first materialistic attitudes (falling into Helle's Pont) developed which so powerfully influenced European culture. It is exactly the sea of Helle that separates 'material' Europe from the 'spiritual' East (where the Sun rises), the sea over which Phryxos escapes from material Ino.

The image associated with this mansion is that of a seated, crowned king, reflecting the warrior energy that has calmed down, has settled and can now be approached. The planetary nature is said to be mainly Mercury with some added Saturn, indicating the more flexible nature of this mansion.

This mansion, like the first one, indicates fieriness, readiness for battle, new beginnings and dedicated quests, to which can be added a more approachable nature and material form. In electional astrology this mansion is good for everything mentioned above but also for approaching authorities and seeking favours.

A good example of how this mansion may work out in a life is the chart of avant-garde poet and art critic Guillaume Apollinaire. Guillaume Apollinaire is the pseudonym of Wilhelm Albert Włodzimierz Apolinary de Kostrowicki, illegitimate child of a Polish mother and an Italian officer born in Rome. Apollinaire travelled a lot but he often lived in France and wrote in French; the ninth house of foreign countries is much emphasized in the chart. He was a poet, a teacher and a writer, one of Picasso's pals and devoted to the surrealist and cubistic avant-garde movement of his time. He coined the term surrealism and was in contact with many leading avant-garde artists.

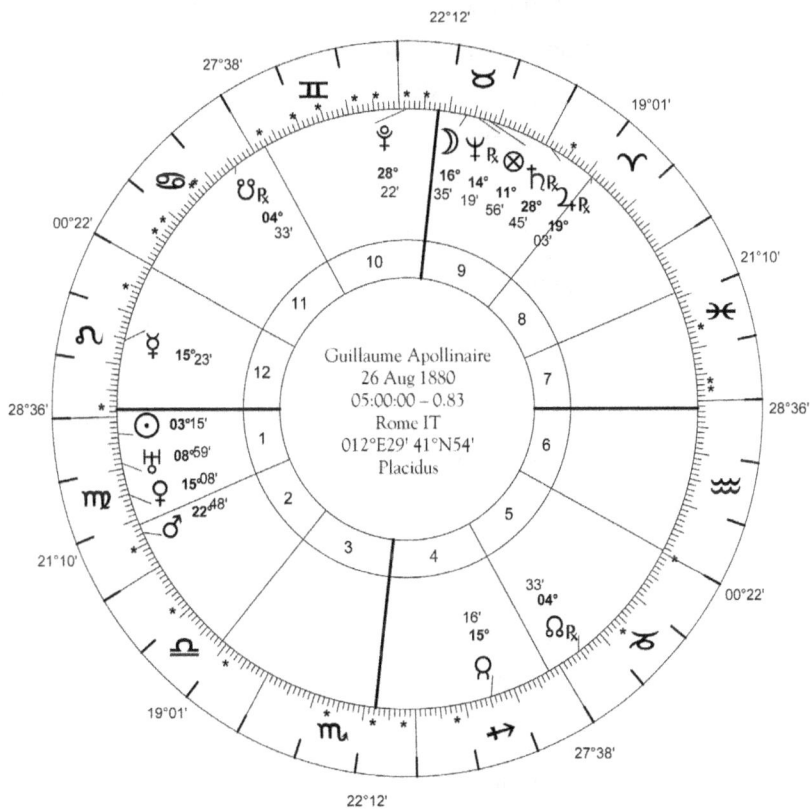

Venus, the planet of the arts, is appropriately Lord 10 of the profession and public activities, and placed in the first house it will be able to manifest clearly. Being in its fall in Virgo, Venus will show its worst side, it will be not very aesthetic or beautiful, but then surrealist and cubistic avant-garde art was not especially concerned about traditional forms of beauty. Virgo is one of Mercury's signs that 'have a voice'. Apollinaire was a poet among painters, not a painter himself. One of his most famous poems is the "Song of the Badly Loved", inspired by an unhappy love affair he had as a young man with a farm girl in the Belgium Ardennes village of Stavelot (there is still a 'Hotel of the badly-loved', Du Mal Aimée in Stavelot). Malefic Saturn is Lord 7 of relationships in the ninth house of foreign countries; it is extremely weak in its detriment and retrograde, and is placed on the Andromeda star Mirach.

His love life tended to be unhappy, but Mirach is a Venus star in the Andromeda constellation, strongly associated with the arts, and it was a source of inspiration too. His ascendant is on powerful Regulus, the most royal star that leads to the throne. Here it can be seen why he was in contact with many artistic celebrities like Picasso and why we still know his name. The Sun is nearby in the first house showing the pen name that made him famous - Apollo is the solar god. His Part of the Sun (Asc + Sun − Moon), also called the Part of the Future, the place where we tend to see the future, is disposed by the optimistic future-thinking planet Jupiter, Lord 5 of creativity, quite appropriate for avant-garde art. The part of the Moon (the Part of Fortune) shows our hunger. It is in the ninth house of ideas and disposed by Venus, the planet of the arts.

The Moon is in its exaltation and by the traditional five-degree orb for cusps is in the tenth house. The Moon will play an important role in his professional life, and this of course reflects the surrealism he so much promoted. Surrealism dissolves form and structure, it wants be fluid and tries to create images of emotional impulses rising up spontaneously. Apollinaire practised automatic writing, noting down what came up without interfering, and you can't get more lunar than that. The lunar mansion Al Butein, with its associations of fiery innovative impulse now cast in a material form, perfectly fits in as the core myth. Mercury's energy describes this mansion. The planet of writing is in the twelfth house and it squares and by antiscion is conjunct the fluid Moon, so yes, through lunar, public activities he will be able to manifest the mansion's promise.

The 28 Mansions – Al Thurayya

3. **Al Thurayya:** 28.53 Taurus - 11.45 Gemini

   Star: The Pleiades

   Arabic letter: Ayn

   Associated name: The Many Little Ones

   Associated planets and energies: Moon/Mars – Pursuit of wealth and success

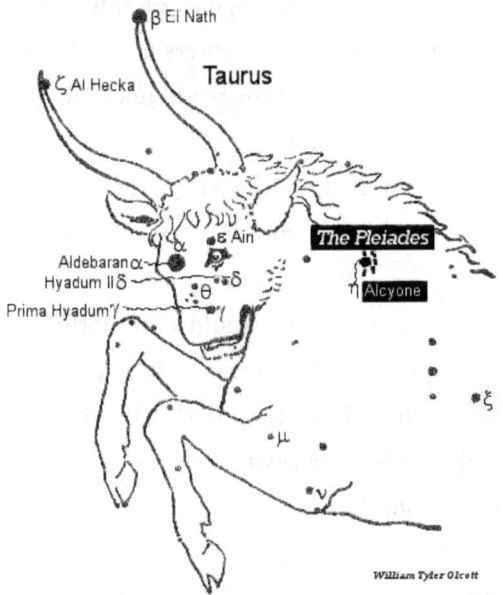

The fires of the first impulse of Aries are left behind in the third mansion of the lunar zodiac, Al Thurayya, which is part of the Taurus constellation. Taurus is much more earthly than Aries, and this is the mansion of probably the most famous star group in the heavens, the Pleiades. The traditional Arabic name of the mansion translates as the 'Many Little Ones' and this points to the fragmentation and the splitting up that the Pleiades represent. This is not a very happy bunch of stars. The Pleiades very much deserve their bad reputation; they are part of the prolonged crisis zone stretching from Algol at 26° Taurus to Aldebaran currently at 10° Gemini. Observing them in the night sky, their signature is telling: their star light is embedded in a nebula of stellar mist, and this is not a positive sign. It shows divine starlight dimmed by matter.

The seven Pleiades stars symbolise the seven sisters who were once married to the seven wise men circling the Pole – a place near God - as the Great Bear, but the sisters were seduced and fell from the divine pole to the more earthly zodiac, far from God. The number seven refers to the seven planets, the seven forces or seals that give form to our life on earth, so the Pleiades represent unhappy bondage to earthly circumstances. This is confirmed by the fact they are the daughters of the Titan (an Earth Giant) Atlas, who was tricked into taking the world upon his shoulders - the idea of heavy material pressures is clear.

The seven sisters were also the virgin companions of Diana, the independent lunar goddess of hunting. As the Moon is the symbol of earthly life, the same central theme can be seen here but in another more positive 'virgin mode'. Diana would have nothing to do with men, and this was also required of her servants, in order to stay purely lunar. According to the myth Orion, the boastful brutish hunter, was always chasing the Pleiades with clear sexual intentions. We see again a theme of disappointing relationships and separation here. The mansion's name clearly echoes the idea of splitting up.

However, the texts on this mansion found in the old books do not seem to mirror this very clearly and they tend to be quite positive, although it is striking that they are mainly positive about very material things, like wealth, possessions and career. It can be seen that this mansion is part of the Taurus constellation, associated with the material level. Naturally there are two sides to this coin. Intensive focus on matter may make you successful and wealthy but it can also cause you to become a prisoner of exactly the material forces pressing you down and making you unhappy. The seven stars refer to the seven planets locking us up in matter, and the connection with the wise men is lost. This is also the myth of Taurus. The bull is Zeus, who brings Princess Europa back to her spiritual origin, so by letting go of material bondage Europa can free herself. Every myth contains a solution to the problems connected to it.

There is some confusion about the nature of the Pleiades, originating in a misunderstood citation from the Holy Bible (Job 38:31): "Canst thou bind the sweet influences of the Pleiades..." The word "sweet" seems to indicate that the Pleiades have a nice positive effect, but this only illustrates the essential meaning of the star group. Sweet is meant here as attractive, as something apparently nice, and indeed the themes of wealth and success the Pleiades mirror are attractive. In their essence, however, they are malefic because of the imprisonment in matter they bring, which cuts you off from higher things. That is exactly why their influence has to be bound! Most typically, attention is always focused on the sweetness, whereas the binding is actually the essential point.

The associated Arabic letter is Ayn. It is connected to the number seventy, ten times seven (the Pleiades' number), exemplifying mulitiplied materially-bound forces (the seven planets), and the letter itself has a fat belly indicating this out-spoken material side. The step in the creational process is called the Universal Nature, again pointing to the same theme. It is logical that a more material Taurus mansion associated with the creative impulse taking form, and connected to Universal Nature, should be concerned with physical things. The planetary rulers in this mansion are the Moon and Mars. The corresponding Vedic mansion is called 'the Knife', showing the same theme of ruthless material ambition, divorce and separation. The mansion's image is a seated woman with the right hand over her head. The woman indicates energy becoming material now (mater = mother), the right hand pointing upward shows the lost connection with the spirit above.

This mansion is good for ruthless ambition, for wealth and material success, although its one-sided material focus will have consequences

and love relationships may suffer. In elections this mansion is favourable for the acquisition of material things and for ambitious enterprises.

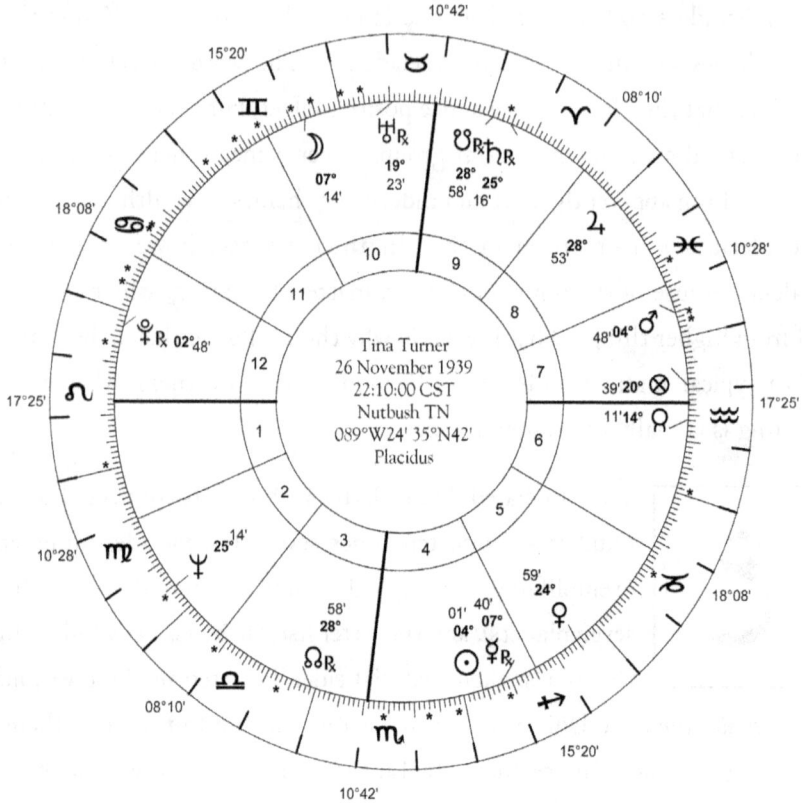

A good example of how Al Thurraya may manifest in a life is given by the chart of Tina Turner, no introduction required. The ruler of her tenth house of the profession is quite appropiately the arty planet Venus, placed in the fifth house of creative activity. This Venus/Lord 10 is in powerful mutual reception with the Great Benefic Jupiter, Lord 5 of creativity, which is very strong in its domicile as Jupiter is placed in the sign where Venus has its exaltation, and Venus is in the domicile of Jupiter. Jupiter makes things big, indicating Tina's very energetic style, and it falls on Scheat, a star in the leg of the Flying Horse Pegasus. Pegasus is on its way to Mount Olympus, a strenuous activity which is anything but calming.

This all-important Jupiter, the Great Benefic, conjoins the Part of Jupiter (Asc + Jupiter − Part of Spirit) by antiscion (position mirrored in the Cancer-Capricorn axis). The Jupiter part is also called the Part of Victory. These parts express the essential energy of a planet, making this is a very, very Jupiter-like Jupiter. Very strong Jupiter Lord 5 of creativity is also in mutual reception with Mars, as Jupiter is in a Water sign and Water has Mars as its elemental ruler and is also in the Face of Mars. Energetic Mars itself is in Pisces, in the sign of Jupiter, giving Jupiter and Mars a strong connection. Mars is in its triplicity, in the right element, it has inner quality; it can manifest in the world easily in the seventh house. And it is on first-magnitude star Deneb, the main star in the Swan, with a Venus character and very much connected to the arts. Begin to get a picture of how she is on stage?

Tina Turner was born a few hours after Full Moon, the moment when the Moon is very weak, and completely filled with solar light, so dominated by the Sun. The Full Moon as the opposition of the masculine Sun and the feminine Moon also points to tensions in relationships. Lord 7, which describes an important partner and/or things happening in relationships, is an extremely weak Great Malefic Saturn retrograde in its fall and conjunct the nasty South Node. Saturn is placed on Al Pherg, a star in the constellation of Pisces; Al Pherg is a star of fateful events. A weaker and nastier Lord 7 could hardly be imagined. For many years Tina Turner suffered from serious, violent abuse inflicted on her by her mentally unstable husband, Ike.

Brought up a Baptist, she has become a Buddhist. Lord 9 of religion is Mars, mentioned above, in mutual reception with this very stong Jupiter, general significator of religion on the Part of Jupiter. She has said that without a spiritual focus she would not have survived all the trouble and abuse she experienced in her life. This also reminds us of the woman in the mansion image, whose hand points upwards. Al Thurraya may take you deeply down into the miseries of matter but the connection with higher things is never totally lost. The Pleiades are said to be seven sisters but actually there are only six bright stars to be seen as one is reputedly invisible and 'lost'. The seventh one has gone back to the divine origin, illustrating the same theme. This is a mansion of heavy material, but we cannot become totally lost in matter. On other points Tina Turner's life has many characteristics of the Pleiades mansion. The energetic ambition, the success, the female power (Diana!), the trouble in her marriage with Ike.

The planetary rulers, Mars and the Moon, are strong enough in angular houses in the chart, so she will be able to manifest the promise of the mansion. The Moon's position in her chart presents a technical complexity. At 7.14 Gemini it is still in the Al Thurrayya mansion, but the Moon is also close to powerful royal Aldebaran, the mighty Bull's Eye, the star 'ruler' of the next mansion. This Alderbaran infuence on the tenth-house Moon considerably contributes to her success. There are two separate star energies working on the Moon here: Aldebaran directly through the star's conjunction and the Pleiades indirectly by the lunar mansion, a phase in the lunar circle of creative steps.

The 28 Mansions – Al Dabaran

4. **Al Dabaran:** 11.45 Gemini – 24.36 Gemini

   Star: Aldebaran, the Bull's Red Eye

   Arabic letter: Hah

   Associated names: The Follower/The Knight

   Associated planets and energies: Mars – Battle/fighting/enmity/material success

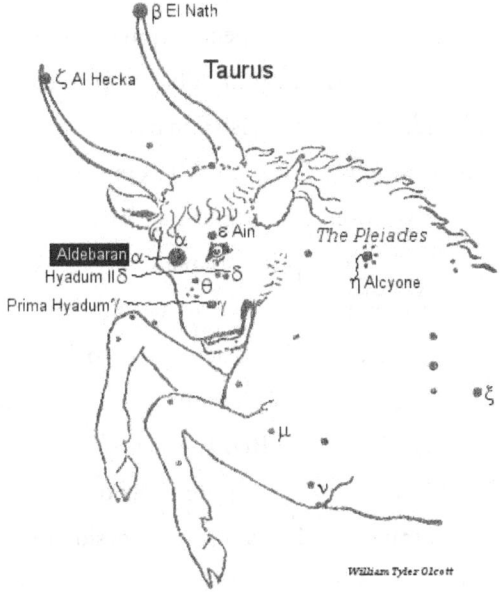

In this mansion we have moved on from the Pleiades on the shoulder of the Bull to the eye, the intensely red and martial star Aldebaran. This is still a Taurus mansion, with all the material associations seen in Al Thurayya, but in a different mode. The meaning of the Arabic name is clear; it is 'the Follower'. It follows the Pleiades, it is the second Taurus mansion and the second phase of the creative impulse, really getting involved in matter. In this second Taurus mansion it is the bright and royal Alderbaran that stands out; the star is the left eye of the Bull and its intense gaze is fixed on earth, symbolising its attention is concentrated on material things.

As we saw in the first Taurus mansion, the Bull is Zeus kidnapping Princess Europa (symbol of the soul), bringing her back to the Isle of

Crete, to the land of her origin. This again is a plan or the solution: it is *through* the inevitable experiences of the material world that the spiritual 'point of departure' of our soul will have to be brought back, for which a severing of material bonds is necessary. This is shown for example by the traditional Spanish *corrida*, very much a Taurus ritual. Of course, following this plan would be the ideal thing to do, but in most cases it is not what we see in life as other characteristics of this mansion of the Bull's Eye come to the fore more clearly. Still all these aspects, higher and lower, can be traced back to the same rich basic symbolism. The simple truth is that you can let go of material bondage in one decisive martial blow, you do not *have* to grasp it, and in this way you will return to Crete immediately.

Aldebaran is a very powerful star and its planetary nature is described purely by Mars. This is an exception as planetary characteristics of stars and constellations are mostly indicated by a combination of two planets. There is a very strong martial combative spirit to be seen here - it will fight for its material success with that red eye obsessively fixed on the earthly world. This mansion of the Red Eye is not very harmonious and its keywords mentioned in the books are quite fiery: discord, fighting, enmity, chaos, ill-will and hindrance. This is a bit too one-sided as the mansion also gives success because of its material orientation, and the Bull can certainly be associated with sensuality. Mars, after all, is the general significator of sexual energy - this is super-fertile Zeus kidnapping a princess.

How a mansion's energy will be manifested in a life is indicated by the dignities of the planetary rulers and their essential and accidental dignities; delineated in the usual way, a lot of essential dignity will indicate an expression of the more positive sides of the mansion. The amount of accidental dignity shows how effectively the promise of the mansion can be realised in the world. In this martial mansion the condition of Mars in the chart should be carefully evaluated, as the planet will have a lot of influence. There is a big difference between the effects of Aldebaran in a chart with Mars in its detriment and a chart with Mars in its domicile. If the Mars energy in the life is not working well - shown by Mars in detriment for example - this will have an effect on the way the mansion shows itself.

The symbolic image associated with this mansion clearly mirrors the martial nature; it is an armed man riding a war horse, holding a snake in his right hand. The snake indicates material desire, which springs forth from the duality for which the snake is a symbol. All in all it is quite appropriate for this material mansion.

 The Arabic letter is Hah, it is associated with the number 8 which is two times earthly 4, and it belongs to the Earth element. This letter also has a 'big belly', indicating the material nature. Again it is said that this is the 'essence in terms of appearance, presence and existence,' so it repeats the meaning of the letter in the second mansion. As it is the first letter of the verb 'to love' it is associated with 'truly God is beautiful and loves beauty' indicating the beauty of material form and 'he loves whomsoever he chooses and he hates whomsoever he wishes to', indicating the martial influence. The creative step is called the *Materia Prima*; in alchemy this is the completely undetermined substance underlying every material form, ready to receive the spirit impulse, so that a concrete form can manifest. The corresponding mansion in Vedic astrology also has a strongly sensual and material nature.

This mansion gives a combative spirit with a lot of fiery energy directed at acquiring material success. It can be associated with argument, battle and enmity; it is not very harmonious, and there is a clear sensual aspect because of the martial energy in the Bull. For elections the texts most appropriately mention all kinds of fighting, hostility, hunting and warfare; it will be clear that this mansion is not good for marriage.

A good example of how Aldebaran may work out in a life is the chart of the American actress Bette Davis. She was famous for her eyes, in fact popular songs were even written about them ('She's got Bette Davis Eyes'). This is a very physical manifestation of the mansion, described by the star in the Bull's Eye staring obsessively down at us on earth. This is no fancy stuff - astrology is about everything in life, including the mundane. Another woman with the Moon in Aldebaran whose eyes made quite some impression is Brigitte Bardot. The other characteristics of this martial Taurus mansion can also be clearly seen playing out in her life - the sensuality and the unharmonious fighting spirit.

Davis' time of birth is quoted in several archives as exactly 21:00, but I would suggest that the real time is 5 minutes earlier giving us the MC on Regulus, the extremely powerful Lion's Heart, which is almost a guarantee of big success. It would also mean that Lord 4 of the family is a weak Saturn in its fall, which seems to fit better with the biographical data about her family. The Sun would become Lord 10 of the profession, strong in its exaltation in the fifth house of creativity, so it seems to be a good idea to make this correction.

Davis was notorious for her direct approach; there was nothing sweet or subtle about her. This is immediately clear in the chart. Lord 1 is Mars in its detriment in Taurus and will show its least attractive sides. It is in the seventh house, very clearly seen in relations with others. It is on Alcyone, the main star of the Pleiades - the Weeping Sisters - giving blindness and disappointments. Venus is nearby but in the next sign, so as Lord 7, of love, walks away from Mars Lord 1 (Davis). This is not exactly promising for stable relationships, and she was married four times.

Mars is also Lord 5 of creativity. Venus, the planet connected with art, is nearby and Lord 10 is in the creative fifth house, so this combination indicates the actress. If there are three indications for some activity in a chart, which may be given in very different ways by a star, a house, a planet, or a planetary part, we can be sure it will manifest. Again this chart raises a technical point, as the Moon is on the powerful star Rigel in the constellation of Orion the Hunter, and Orion is a rough guy, lacking

The 28 Mansions – Al Dabaran

subtlety. He certainly has a direct approach, and this fits in perfectly with what we know about Bette Davis. However, the Moon is also in the Aldebaran mansion, so which star is the Moon connected to?

These are just two perspectives to bear in mind. As with every planet, part or angle, the Moon may or may not be on a star, which would provide more important information about how it will work out in the life. At the same time the Moon will always have a position in her 'own' lunar zodiac. Davis' Moon at 16.47 Gemini is not really very close to Aldebaran but it does partake of the Aldebaran effect, as these energies are carried forward by the Moon through the zodiac.

The effects of Aldebaran can be seen clearly in her life, modified by the planets' positions: the eyes, the quarreling, the marital problems, the fiery approach, the success and the sensuality, her typical 'baddy' roles.

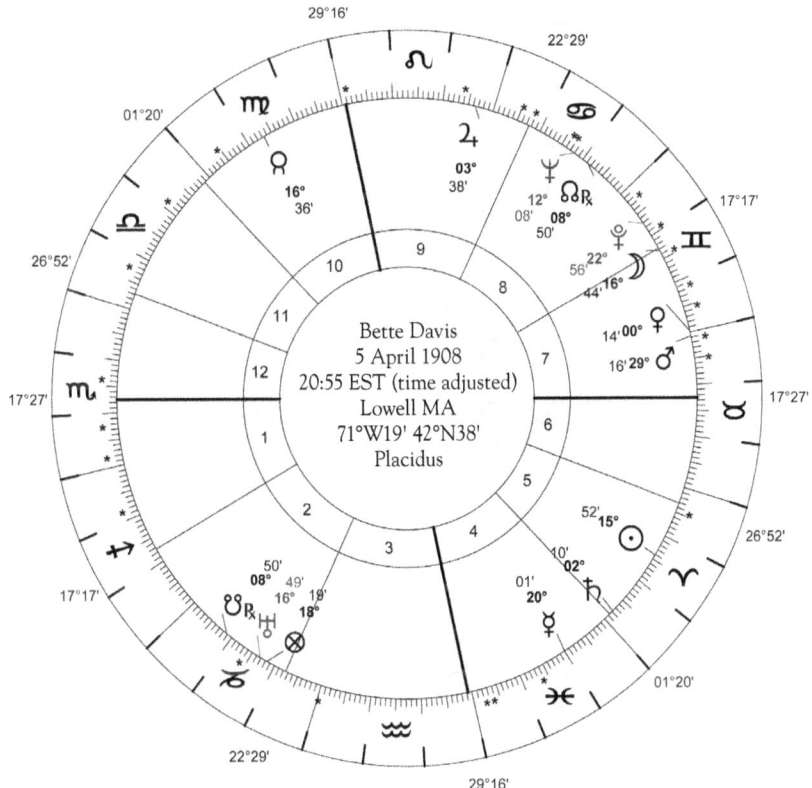

As Mars is essentially weak the nastier sides will come out more strongly. The martial fire in the mansion will tend to manifest more in endless conflicts. Mars is very strong in an angular house so it will be seen clearly, particularly in relationships. Brigitte Bardot's Mars is essentially stronger than Davis' Mars, so in her chart Aldebaran will work out less radically. Bardot's Mars is more able to control this mansion's fiery energies.

---

5. **Al Haqa:** 24.36 Gemini - 7.28 Cancer

   Star: Meissa, Orion's Head

   Arabic letter: Ghayn

   Associated names: The White Spot/The King's Head

   Associated planets and energies: Mars/Mercury – Favours given/control by thinking

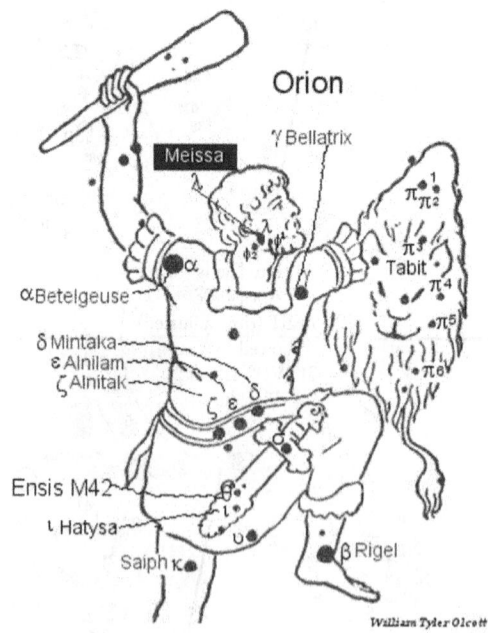

The name of this fifth lunar mansion is Al Haqa, the meaning of which is 'the White Spot' and this is a bit mysterious. One possible explanation is

the placement of its ruling star Meissa in the head of Orion; the emphasis in this mansion is clearly on the head. This is confirmed by the associated image, which is also a head. It may be that the whiteness mentioned in 'the White Spot' points to calm thinking, which is the core theme of this mansion. The constellation of Orion in which this mansion is found has much to do with the story of the rough and violent hunter, so a tension is indicated by the emphasis on the head controlling the rough hunter.

After the Great Bear, Orion is probably the best-known constellation among star-spotters as it is very large, marked out by a girdle of three stars and by bright Rigel, Betelgeuse and Bellatrix. You can hardly miss it if you look up, and as always this has a symbolic connotation too. Astrology is a form of knowledge based on quality and symbol; we live in a cosmos structured by these principles. The sheer size of Orion indicates out that this is an important theme in the life of human beings. Some traditions even say that souls on their way to earthly life pass through Orion first. This all provides information about the nature of this huge constellation.

Orion is the successful hunter who was able to catch and kill all animals and this would feed his pride. He forgot that he was only a limited creature and not some god, and this was not appreciated by the gods, as could be expected. They decided to teach him a lesson and sent down the Scorpion, an animal he could not beat. Orion died from the poisonous sting of its tail. It is also said that Orion was made only of ox hide and that he was nothing more than a rough bundle of material instincts and desires, lacking any kind of higher guidance or connection. He is the hubris of the human ego, fostering the illusion that it can violently force its hand on reality.

So the core theme in Orion is clear: it has to do with great success, but pride and arrogance will be punished by the sting of the Scorpion. The interesting thing is that the star Meissa mentioned as the ruling star is not among the Orion stars given in the old texts as astrologically relevant; all the relevant stars are placed on the girdle, the sword, the feet or the shoulders. Meissa however is found in the head indicating an emphasis on the control by cool thinking over the wild animal impulses of the arrogant Hunter that is composed only of matter. All the martial impulse of Aldebaran in the previous mansion of the red burning eye of the Bull, the creative impulse coming down into matter, is controlled and disciplined here. This is one of the few mansions in the Arabian system associated with a non-zodiacal constellation, indicating the importance of Orion.

The tension between the Hunter nature and the controlling head is reflected in the planets ruling it: Mars of violent action and Mercury of cool, rational thinking. The symbolic image of the head as mentioned above repeats the same theme of rulership and control by doing the correct thing and controlling impulses.

The associated Arabic letter Ghayn seems to give a very graphic picture of this mansion's essence, as the point above the letter repeats the symbolic image of a white spot (star) controlling the mass below. It is said to symbolise the perfection of the apparent (material) image, repeating the control of material, baser impulses by rational thinking. It belongs to the Earth element befitting the gross Orion nature and its number is 100 - reflecting the perfection of 1, but multiplied as manifesting in matter. The creative step is the Universal Body, the term 'Body' reflecting the ongoing materialization.

The fifth house in the Hindu system is also an Orion house and emphasizes strong instincts, passions and a rough nature.

The fifth mansion is connected to thinking and the mind, and is used to control strong instinctive, material impulses. It is good for asking favours as the wise head is a central image here; the passionate hunting for the satisfaction of the desires remains important.

A good chart illustrating how Al Haqa may work out in a life is that of Prince William, the current Duke of Cambridge and probably the future

The 28 Mansions – Al Haqa

King of England. The Sun is immediately obvious in this chart, as the general significator of kings is very prominent in the seventh house and by antiscion is conjunct the descendant. It illustrates his role as a royal; the seventh house is the house of others in general and not only of love relationships. It is part of a New Moon, so strongly connected to the Moon of the people, also showing that a new cycle of relating to the people will be starting with him. With a view to what has happened, this is quite understandable.

The New Moon by antiscion on the descendant opposes the ascendant, so the royal role he will be playing is in a very tense relationship with his personal life on the ascendant. The Moon is also the general significator of the mother, moving away from this Sun. The problem with the mother is confirmed by the condition of Mars/Lord 10 (the mother), very weak in its detriment in Libra and on the malefic star of separation and falling, Vindemiatrix. Lord 4 of the family root is a very strong Venus in Taurus, but it is on the super-malefic disaster star Algol, showing trouble in the family.

Jupiter/Lord 1, symbolising the most out-spoken Prince William himself, is on the MC, repeating the prominent public position given by the New Moon. But it opposes the IC of the family showing his doubts about the family and the position it gave him. The Part of Fortune or the Part of the Moon, our hunger, opposes the royal New Moon, suggesting he hungers for other than these public solar things. Nevertheless, he will not walk away easily as Jupiter Lord 1 is in station, in a fixed sign; he will fulfill his duties, despite all the tensions given by the chart. Jupiter/Lord 1, Prince William 'in his life', is on the boundary of the sign. He can see the other side, the other sign and he may have considered moving over, but he does not enter the other sign by further retrogradation. Jupiter will become stationary and turn around, staying in the sign.

The lunar mansion fits in very nicely. It is all about the head of a king taking cool decisions, controlling his more instinctive impulses. To see how the mansion will work out for him the planetary rulers Mars and

Mercury have to be evaluated, always of course in the context of the whole chart. This again reflects the split. Mars, anger and more basic impulses, is in a very bad condition in its detriment in Libra. Mars also refers to the mother as Lord 10, the anger and frustration connected to her fate. Mercury, the clear-thinking part, is in very good condition in Gemini on powerful Aldebaran and Lord of the seventh house of dealing with others. A balance will be found; the head of the king, so strong in essential dignity, will be able to control the anger and frustration and make a disciplined decision.

His younger brother Harry did walk out. Harry's chart looks like that of his older brother on several points but he does not have the same solar

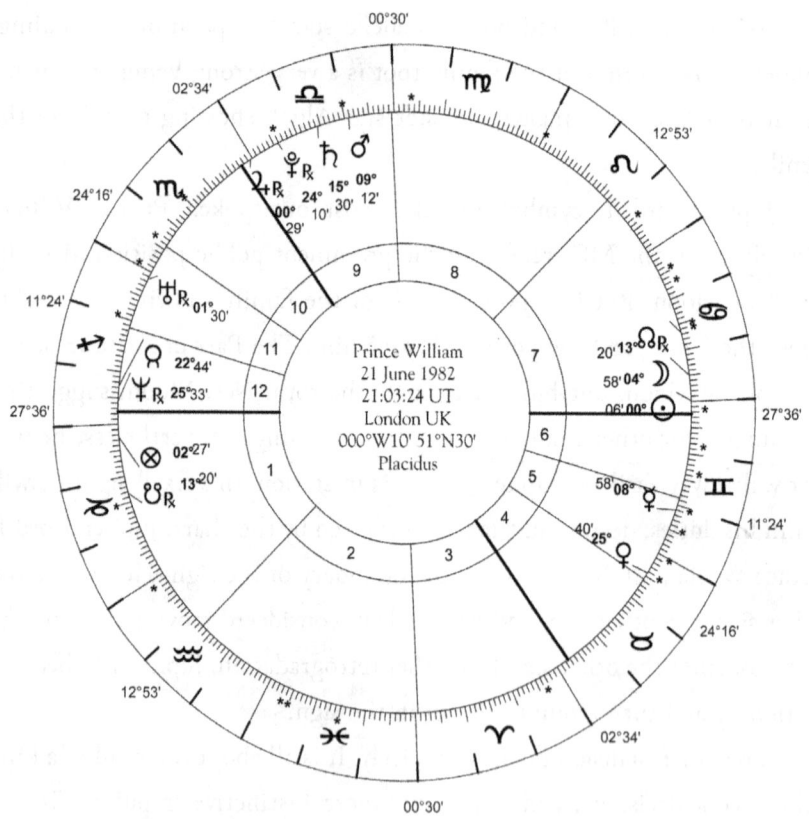

power in an angular house, and he was not destined to be king. And of course his Moon is in another mansion, which is quite revealing. Harry's lunar mansion is Al Botein, the Ram's Belly, the second Aries mansion. This is still a mansion of raging Aries fire although it has calmed down somewhat. Comparing the two brothers' mansions it clearly shows Harry is the one who would tend to break with his family and position. The lunar mansion can be seen as a central crystallisation point in the chart giving some very basic decisions, experiences, motivations, attitudes, tendencies, situations and events. One of the keywords of Al Botein is reconciliation, which shows us that keywords have to be handled with utmost care. Cookbook astrology is always to be avoided.

---

6. **Al Hana:** 7.28 Cancer - 20.20 Cancer

   Star: Alhena, Pollux' Foot

   Arabic letter: Kha

   Associated names: The Mark/Little Star of Great Light/The Pair

   Planets and energies: Mercury/Venus – Sympathy/love/attraction

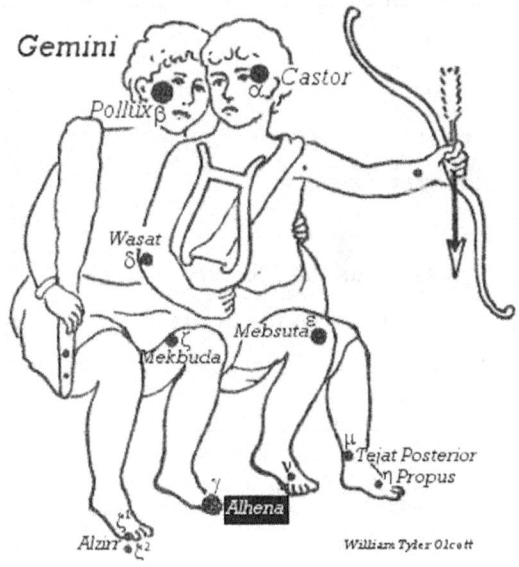

The sixth lunar mansion falls in the constellation of Gemini and it is called Al Hana after its star Alhena on Pollux's foot, which is Arabic for 'a mark'; the star is also associated with a brand burnt in and even quite literally with afflictions to the feet. The feet symbolise the point where we are connected to the earth, to the realities of life, and this may be quite a painful process as we all know. The affliction and the tension in the background here originates in this point where the earth is touched. Gemini, the constellation of the brothers Castor and Pollux, at the deepest level is associated with the two polar energies of life on earth. Castor and Pollux are brothers, referring to two parts of the human being which are very strongly connected.

Castor is the mortal brother, the part of us more earth-bound, and Pollux is the immortal brother, the part aiming at a connection with 'above', with returning to the divine source. We are spirits in a material world, which is the cause of a lot of problems. The brothers symbolise a basic pair, a duality in a tense relationship, 'two souls in one breast'. They are also great warriors involved in the struggles of life, mythologically told as the battles the brothers engage in. In one of these battles mortal Castor is killed, but even then they remain connected, Pollux lives with his brother in Hades for a part of the year and Castor goes to be with his brother on Mount Olympus for another part of the year. Everything here illustrates that these two poles are closely connected but have different meanings, and this connection is the reason the name 'Little Star of Great Light' is associated with it.

The ruling planets Venus and Mercury mirror this very closely, Venus showing the loving bond between the brothers and Mercury as the planet of splitting up into material detail, pointing out their necessary difference and separation. This painful process explains the name of 'a mark burnt in', associated with Alhena. A pair can never be a total unity, a pair can only be in complementary relationship and it should not come as a surprise that this mansion is very much associated with relationships. The symbolic image gives us a man and a woman, two people embracing; this mansion is very positive as everything is connected to love, attraction and friendship.

 The associated Arabic letter is Kha. Its number is 600, which is 10 x 30, doubled. The letter is said to symbolise the eternal good in Sufi brotherhoods, because of the love associated with it, and it corresponds to the taste of light, as love is the doorway to unity. The creative step is called 'The Form', illustrating that the connection of two poles is the creative principle giving you the form of things. In Hindu astrology the sixth mansion is an Orion mansion, so it does not correspond to this Arabian Gemini mansion. Although there are striking similarities between both systems they are not the same, as they have a different starting-point and a different number of mansions.

This mansion is very good for love, friendship and attraction. It is not however good for things that need slow, stable development like crops or buildings.

The example chart is not a natal chart but an election, so this is a good point to explain some of the principles and how to use the mansions in electional astrology. There are several forms of electional astrology: a quick choice for an optimal moment to do something, an election by horary, and a more elaborate election in which the natal chart is also taken into account. As the whole mansion system is based on the daily movement of the Moon, giving the general ambience, it is possible to pick a favourable day for an action. It would be a good idea for example to plan a romantic date when the Moon is in this sixth mansion, in the thirteenth 'love' mansion Al Awwa, or at least avoid mansions not too good for harmonious connections.

Another kind of election is done by horary, when clients ask you to find the optimal time to start some activity. You can use a horary chart if the situation does not permit a complete election because the client cannot determine the time of starting the action exactly (as is often the case in medical contexts) or if it is sufficient to give a less detailed time period, like 'between 12 and 23 January' or 'after mid-November'. In the chart of the horary question the relevant significators are moved forwards to check when they will reach a strong position and timing is done symbolically as usual, one degree of movement standing for a time unit; quite often in elections 1 degree = 1 week. This means the lunar mansions are not very important in horary elections - what counts mainly is a strong relevant significator.

In the most complete elections lunar mansions do play a role. This kind of election can be made for opening a shop, marrying, or starting a business. It will lead to a very specific optimal time, calculated down to the minute, and the client's natal chart plays an important role. You will use the natal chart to select the planets that should be strong in the elected chart. For a business, natal Lord 10 should be strong in the election and natal Lord 1, which is the person, obviously cannot be weak. The next step is to move to the election and pick a period, if possible, during which the general significator of the action is strong. So for a marriage, Venus should be in Pisces, Libra or Taurus; for a bookshop Mercury should be in Gemini. These are optimal positions but there are other strong possibilities.

The time window given by your client will in most cases limit your possibilities. In the election chart the relevant houses and their rulers should be strong, and strong appropriate fixed stars should be placed on relevant angles and house rulers; harmful aspects should be avoided. This is quite complex so concessions will have to be made; electing is a fine balancing act. Putting the Moon in an appropriate lunar mansion is one of the things to be taken into account, as the Moon gives us the general ambience; this is not a factor to be ignored. It is however important to be realistic. In some cases an inappropriate lunar mansion will have to be accepted if other relevant factors are strong. Practical experience shows

The 28 Mansions – Al Hana

that things will tend to fall into place if you are searching in the right direction and aligning yourself with the cosmic currents.

A good example is the following election made for the opening of a restaurant in Vienna. First the relevant significators were extracted from the owner's natal chart. Lord 1 in the natal chart was Saturn and in the time-window given by the client Saturn was exalted in Libra, which is fine. Unfortunately, Jupiter was natal Lord 10 of public activities and natal Lord 11 of the money made by these activities, and Jupiter is weak in its detriment in Gemini. This has to be accepted as we cannot wait forever. If the chart provides enough compensation for this weakness, it is not a fundamental problem. In the election chart Mars, the general significator of restaurants,

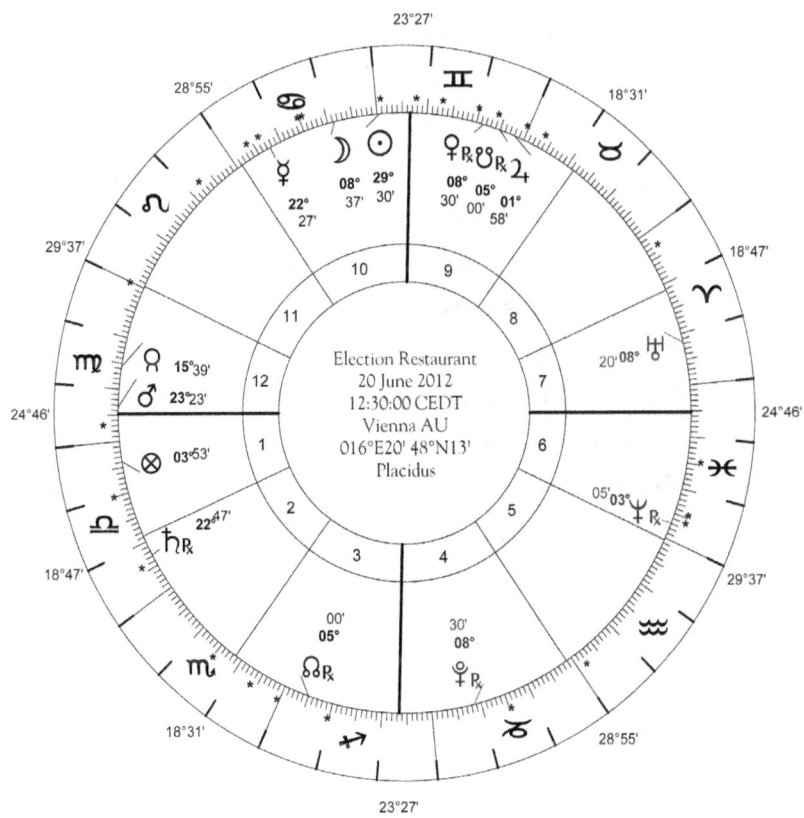

was put on the ascendant - a lot of heating and cutting going on there - so this is appropriate, although it is not in a sign where it is strong, as this was impossible to organise.

There is however a lot of strength in other parts of the chart. Mercury is election Lord 1 and Lord 10 making it extremely important. It has a lot of power in the tenth house being placed on Pollux, the star of royal success. The Moon, the general significator of feeding and caring, is very strong in its domicile in the tenth house and by antiscion (position mirrored in the 0° Cancer-0° Capricorn axis) right on the MC. The Moon is election Lord 11 of earnings, very nice. Also in the tenth house is the Sun on powerful Betelgeuse, and the MC itself is on first magnitude Capella, the main star in the Wagon-driver providing speed. Saturn, natal Lord 1 is very strong, exalted in the second house of money and on the powerful royal star Spica.

Yes, there are downsides too. Natal Lord 2 of money is not strong, being retrograde near the South Node, but it is so placed that it falls by antiscion on strong Mercury and it is on royal Aldebaran, a great success star. The Moon as Lord 11 of earnings is in opposition with Pluto, this could not be avoided, but it is so strong it can take this. The lunar mansion Al-Hana as the general ambience fits in very well. It is a mansion of connection, attraction and friendship - who would not want that in a restaurant? The ruling planets Venus and Mercury are conjunct by antiscion in the tenth house, so the mansion's potential can easily manifest. A few years after making the election when I was in Vienna to give a seminar, I had the experience of having dinner in my own election.

The 28 Mansions – Al Dhira

7. **Al Dhira:** 20.20 Cancer – 3.11 Leo

   Star: Castor (the Mortal Twin's Head)

   Arabic letter: Qaf

   Associated names: The Forearm

   Planets and energies: Mercury – Business success

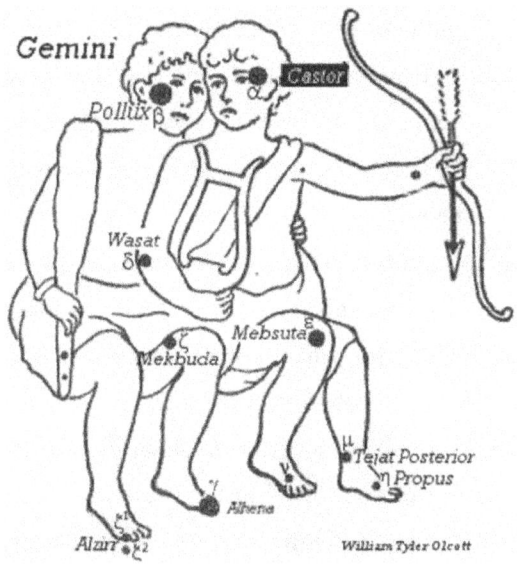

This seventh mansion is called Al Dhira, Arabic for 'the Forearm' and it is said that the Arabs saw the foreleg of a great lion here. This cannot be directly connected to our astrological symbolism or a star but it can be seen as an indication of the worldly power and success given by this mansion. This seventh mansion is still part of Gemini, with similarities to Al Hana, and can be associated with the same mythological story – we will not repeat the myth here. The emphasis in this mansion is totally different, however, as can be seen clearly in the picture above. In Al Hana, the focus was on the foot of the immortal twin Pollux and the central theme was the connection of the poles, highlighting love, affinity and friendship.

As this concerned immortal Pollux the orientation was upward, and therefore this mansion had a very positive meaning. In that part of the constellation the bond between the brothers stood out, reflected in the planetary rulers Venus and Mercury. In this second Gemini mansion the mortal part of the Twins comes to the fore. The descriptive star is Castor, placed at the beginning of the mansion, its 'gate' we might say, although Pollux is also found in the mansion. The lower mortal tendency is shown here by Castor's planetary nature which is Mercurial. Mercury is the pragmatic energy, and does not care too much for higher things or ethics.

The Twins are great warriors and tamers of horses so they have the power and motivation to fight for what they want in the world. Combining all this, the central theme associated with this mansion is clear. It is business success. The worldly power of the Twins given by their symbolism of the 'founding' polarity of reality is oriented here towards practical and pragmatic goals; with the mortal brother here we forget about higher connections and just go for what yields the most profits. The symbolic image is a man clothed in robes with his arms extended to heaven in the manner of prayer. This is not as clear as we might wish, but it seems to illustrate the blessing from above leading to success. The extended arms could be a literal picture of Al Dhira, the Fore-Arm representing the power to act.

The letter in this mansion is 'Qaf'. Its number is 100 and its element Water; it is said to be connected to inner vision.

The complete number 100 – full force deployed in the world – here probably also points to the fact that we have come to the end of the first quarter of seven mansions which contains the principles of the cosmos. In this first quarter, formulated as creative steps, we move from the 'First Intellect' in Al Sharatain to 'the Throne' in Al Dhira. The Throne is prepared here for the ruler to sit on so that the king can exercise his power. The second and third quarters of the cycle (the eighth to the twenty-first mansion) refer to the middle level of the cosmos that passes on the creative energies. These are the intermediate phases in the creative process, the spheres of the planets and the elements. The fourth quarter of the last seven mansions is said to refer to the 'composed beings', like animals and men living on earth, composed of all these forces. So the further you move in the cycle of creation, the more complex the creative phase is.

The corresponding Vedic mansion is also described by Castor and Pollux and also shows a strong influence of Mercury.

This mansion is very good for success in business. It is good for gain and wealth, for friendship and alliances and for asking favours.

The example chart is in this case not a natal or an electional chart but a progression of the Moon through the mansions. As the cycle of the mansions is very much a cycle of development, the movement of the secondary progressed Moon through the mansions can be very helpful in prognosis. The secondary progressed Moon moves about the length of a lunar mansion in a year, so often there is a transition to a new mansion in making a prognosis for a client, giving important indications about what is going on. Note however, it should be interpreted in the context of the other factors; the planets describing the mansions are important as they show how positive the mansion will work out in the life. The progressions we look at are those in Donald Trump's chart at the time he won the US presidency in November 2016.

Donald Trump's natal chart was analysed in Chapter 6 of my book *Fixed Stars in the Chart* and it is an extremely powerful chart, one of the most powerful I have ever seen. As could be expected his progressions (for the angles, ascendant and MC primary directions, as only planets make a secondary movement through the signs) in November 2016 activated a lot of these strong positions. The first thing striking the eye is the Sun, Lord 1 in his natal chart moving over Regulus, the most royal star of the royal stars, which leads to the throne. It is true that the Sun is leaving its domicile, which is weakening, but by entering Virgo the sign's ruler Mercury is activated, and in Trump's natal chart Mercury by antiscion conjuncts the Sun, general significator of kings, placed in the tenth house of profession on the North Node, the area of growth and expansion!

His ascendant is moving over the secondary progressed Jupiter, also growth and expansion. Of course, the secondary progressed Jupiter moves far too slowly to be taken into account in prediction but if it is aspected by a faster factor, as in this case, it does count. This ascendant-Jupiter conjunction is on another extremely powerful royal star, Spica, which has the reputation of taking you to a higher position than you could ever have dreamt of. The Part of the Sun, indicated in the chart by the reversed

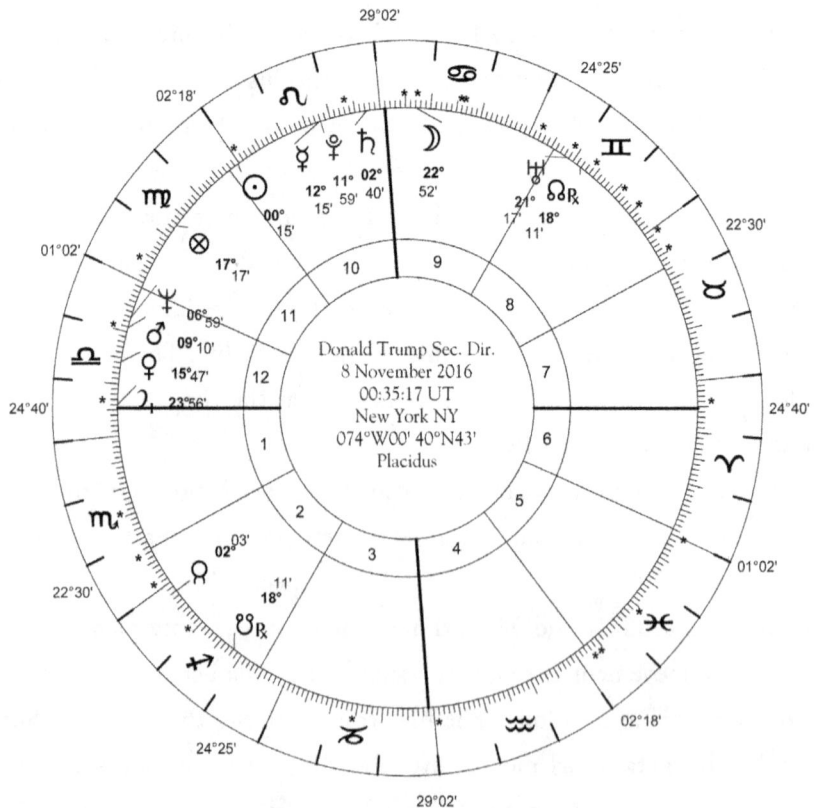

Taurus symbol is just entering Scorpio, activating Scorpio's ruler Mars, again very powerfully placed on his natal ascendant, which falls on Regulus.

The Part of the Sun is calculated by the formula Asc + Sun − Moon (the reversed formula of the Part of Fortune, which is the Part of the Moon), and its progressed position is composed of the primary direction of the ascendant and the secondary progressions of the luminaries, the Sun and Moon. Note, because of its calculation formula, it is moving *backwards* through the signs. For clarity, progressions/directions give the main line of development in a life; the six most important factors are the Sun and Moon, the Parts of the Luminaries (Part of the Sun and the Part of the Moon) and the direction of the angles, ascendant and MC. Also to be analysed are conjunctions with fixed stars, ingresses into new signs or terms and aspects on natal and other progressed factors. You do not need much more to give you a clear idea of what is going on. So three of these factors activate very powerful natal positions and royal fixed stars, and the movement of the Moon only confirms this success. It is on Pollux, another royal star and the immortal Twin! The progressed Moon is also conjunct his natal Lord 10 of profession.

Now that we have the context of the progressions/directions, the lunar mansion can be interpreted. At 22.49 Cancer the secondary progressed Moon is moving from Al Hana to Al Dirah; for the past twelve months Trump has been doing a Venus/Mercury, 'connecting' Al Hana things. The natal position of Venus and Mercury are strong so it will be effective. Now that he is elected as president the Moon moves into Al Dhira, the mansion of success. Its ruler Mercury is very strong in his natal chart, conjunct the Sun/Lord 1 on the North Node in the tenth house on powerful Capella (by antiscion). This is quite impressive and shows how the Moon through the mansions can be effectively used as a prediction instrument as part of a bigger picture.

The Lunar Mansions Guide

Second quarter of Seven Mansions

8. **Al Natrah:** 3.11 Leo - 16.02 Leo

   Star: Praesepe (the Empty Crib)

   Arabic letter: Kaf

   Associated names: The Gap/The Raptor

   Planets and energies: Mars/Moon – Rulership/dominance

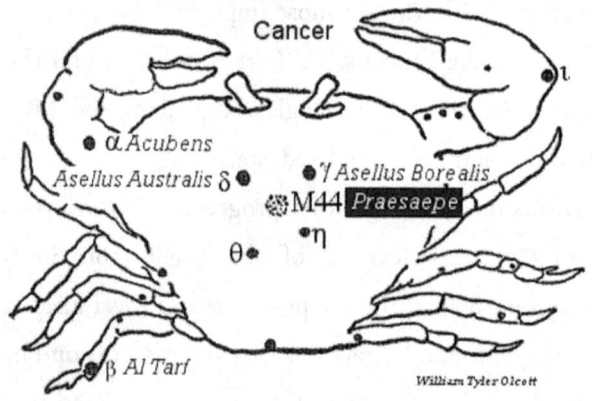

In this eighth mansion we enter the second quarter of the cycle which reverts to the archetypical basic model of the lunar mansion cycle overlaid on the solar sign zodiac; this is also the beginning of the fourth sign, Cancer. In a solar season of three signs there are seven mansions, but this is only so in the theoretical archetypical blueprint; the precession of the mansions has moved forward as explained in Part 1 and Al Natrah does not start at 0° Cancer in the tropical zodiac in our lifetime. Nevertheless, we can read meanings from the position of the mansions in the archetypical zodiacal blue-print; the start of Cancer is the summer solstice and the Sun is at its highest point, so this is a sign of power.

The name of this mansion Al Natrah means 'the Gap' in Arabic, and it is clear where it comes from, as the Gemini constellation has been left behind and this is Cancer. The star ruling this mansion is Praesepe 'the

Heart of Cancer', also called the Empty Crib and that is what 'the Gap' refers to. In mythology the Crab is crushed by the hero Hercules because it is biting his heel, trying to distract him while is he is busy killing the monstrous Hydra, a very important job. The Crab, always going with the flow of the emotions and wishes, is a symbol for exactly that, following desires which distract you from your main job.

Praesepe, the Crib, is empty; it is a gap, because there is no guiding higher principle here, only the Cancerian waters of desire. The central theme here is falling into the gap or not; Praesepe has a very bad name and this reputation is well-deserved and proven in practice. There is a real danger that the desire nature takes over and this often can be associated with power, success and ambition.

The planets ruling here are quite appropriately the Moon, emotional impulse, and Mars, sudden action. The keywords are connected to power, dominance, alliance and victory, confirmed very clearly by the remarkable mansion image. This image is an eagle with the head of a human being; a picture of predatory striking-power. The question is: does the human head guide it or is it guided? Handling power and ambition seems to be the central theme, quite in line with the story about Hercules and the Crab.

The Arabic letter is Kaf, its number is 20 so the duality of 2 which creates desire, multiplied into manifestation by the 10, means it belongs most appropriately to the Water element and it is associated with creating. This confirms what was said above, as Cancer is the free-flowing desire to live, to grasp life. The creative step is called the 'Pedestal' or 'the Two Feet', showing the entry into the second, more physical quarter. The first quarter of pure principles is left behind, and now we are coming down into the intermediate phases in the Two Feet touching earth. The parallel Vedic mansion is said to be good for success and wealth too.

According to the Sufi metaphysician Ibn El Arabi, the Shaikh Al Akbar, the 'greatest master', this mansion/creative step is called the Two Feet as here at the beginning of the second quarter for the first time both sides of God manifest, not only his Mercy but also his Wrath. The reason is that the distance from the unity of the beginning is increasing, and the further away we get from divine origin, the darker it becomes. It could be said that the duality of matter is introduced here. The idea that Cancer represents the free-flowing water of desire for life fits in very well. At this point we enter life and we want it all, and at the opposite point in Capricorn we leave. The function of these creative steps can be seen clearly; if you have your Moon in the associated mansion, your being is very much connected to this phase in the creative process.

This mansion is good for conquering, victory, wealth, power and ambition (also in elections), this success is said to extend to marriage. Controlling, handling power and developing a clear focus are the central themes here.

A good example of how Al Natrah may work out in a life is the natal chart of Queen Elizabeth II of England. The first thing we notice in her chart is the South Node on the ascendant. The nodal axis is the draconic axis, which is the duality energy, the axis of creation. At the North Node you come in, thirsting for experience in life, and at the South Node you go out, life is taken away. So basically it means the Queen has to sacrifice her personal life on the ascendant; the expansive North Node on the descendant of other people shows what she will be doing all the time – meeting and dealing with others. What is conjunct the South Node has to be sacrificed, otherwise one will suffer a lot.

On the MC, the highest point in the chart, is Saturn Lord 1 - the Queen 'in her life situation' - so she is very visible up there. The ruler of the first house is the person (not the Sun, which is too general). She is up there in a fixed sign and Saturn is not the planet of change, so she will embody

The 28 Mansions – Al Natrah

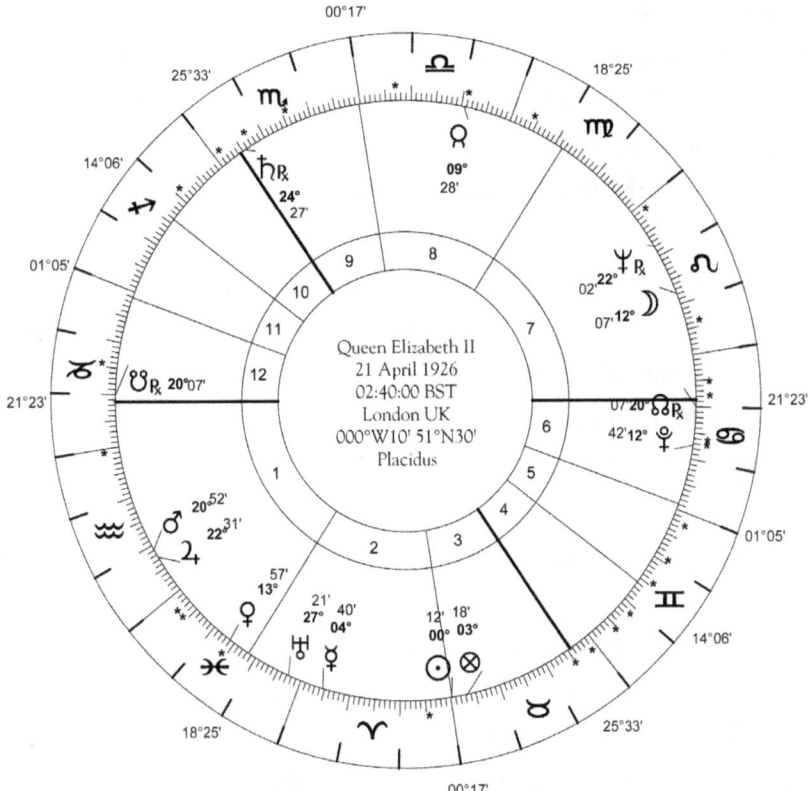

tradition - she is even moving backwards. Lord 10 of the profession, Mars, is also fixed and placed in her first house so this is a kind of a reception by houses ('in mundo' reception), Lord 1 in the tenth house and Lord 10 in the first house connecting person and job very closely. Lord 10 in this fixed sign is conjunct Jupiter, which extends the matter, so she will be a stayer in the job. This is confirmed by the Sun, the general significator of crowned heads, which is in the very first degree of Taurus, the most fixed of the fixed signs!

The Part of Fortune indicating our hunger, or the things which we can't do enough, is in the third of routine duties. That's very nice as she does them a lot, and she wants them to be done well. She is also good at it, as elegant harmonious Venus is the ruler of the third house in its exaltation (exaggeration) in Pisces on the powerful Jupiter star Achernar. The royal Sun is right on the cusp of the third house and the Part of the royal Sun is in Libra, so it has Venus /Lord 3 as its dispositor. A dispositor of a part shows in which area of life the energy of the Part is oriented, and the Part of the Sun is directed again at Venus, doing routine things! No wonder she has so much stamina; this nice Venus in exaltation makes it all quite graceful and as it should be done. Just as in the chart of her grandson William, Lord 1 is in opposition with the family roots that put her up there and of course she will have had her doubts about it all, but duty would have called.

The lunar mansion Al Natrah, the Gap, fits in fine. It is all there, the high position handling power, and the control and discipline to do it. There have been many other royals who allowed their position to run away with them, to abuse it to satisfy their personal desires or act out their frustration with dire consequences, but the Queen remains unperturbed. Neither of the planetary rulers of Al Natrah, the Moon and Mars, are essentially strong but they're not especially weak either; accidentally they are powerfully placed in an angular house enabling the whole theme of Al Natrah to manifest. Like other astrological factors a mansion can work out in many ways; it is the specific individual context given in the chart that shows us exactly what effect it will have. Other people with the Moon in Al Natrah will handle it in a different way and it is most instructive to compare these cases.

9. **Al Tarf:** 16.02 Leo – 28.54 Leo

   Star: Al Terf (the Lion's Glance)

   Arabic letter: Jim

   Associated names: The Lion's Eyes/The Blinded

   Planets and energies: Saturn/Mars – Loss/frustration/confrontation with authorities

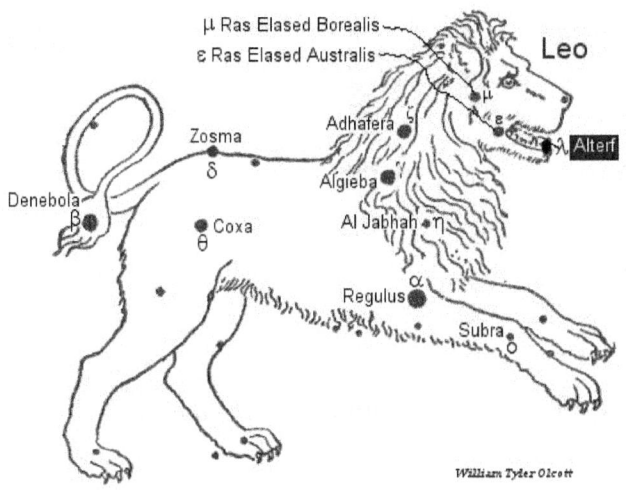

The name of the ninth mansion may cause confusion as it often called Al Tarf 'the Eyes' and also 'the Glance of the Lion'. The star referred to here however is Al Terf and not Altarf which is another star, admittedly not too far away. But Altarf is on the legs of Cancer, so has nothing to do with this mansion as we have left Cancer behind now. Here we are entering the Leo constellation and it has no less than four mansions, the Eyes, the Heart, the Back and the Tail. Quite appropriately Leo is big! All the mansions have different meanings and effects, determined by the specific part of Leo they cover and in which the descriptive star is found, but at the background in all the mansions is the myth of Leo.

Leo is the Nemean Lion, and the first of the twelve labours of Hercules was to kill this vicious, fierce and very dangerous beast. The hero Hercules, symbolising man as he ought to be, succeeded in killing it, stripping off the skin and wearing the skin of the Lion's head on his own head. This is a sign he has conquered the evil of the Lion and got rid of a burning, merciless ambition, a lust for power, and a desire to be admired. Leo wants an immortal name and will struggle for the power it needs to achieve that. The killing of the Lion here is the way to solve its problems. It means you have to sacrifice burning ambition, but after that you can still use the Leo energy, shown by the skin of the Lion's head worn by Hercules. The difference is it is no longer using you - you're not destroyed by ambition any more.

There is a similarity with the previous mansion, in that in Al Natrah the central point was concentration on your main task in order not be distracted. Here the focus is on strong ambition and its possible dire consequences. The ruling planets, the two malefics Saturn and Mars, indicate that this is not a very fortunate house as it is all about the glance of the Lion - the confrontation with the vicious monster is highlighted here. Its keywords are very negative: loss, falling, disgrace and confrontations. Clearly there can be a strong tendency to use the Leo energy in the wrong way. The image confirms this tendency, it is a man covering his eyes; consciousness is darkened.

The name 'the Glance of the Lion' shows another important effect of this mansion: if a lion glances at you, it means you are facing it. You have come across it and indeed that is quite a dangerous thing, so covering your eyes is an understandable reaction. The point is you are confronting this fierce beast, and the emphasis in this part of the story of the Nemean lion is on the fighting; the essence is the power struggle with the authorities. People with this configuration may tend to defy the powers that be and can be quite provocative about this. The power beast Leo can certainly represent mainstream ideas too, and fighting mainstream ideas and the powers that be could lead to the frustrations mentioned.

The 28 Mansions – Al Tarf

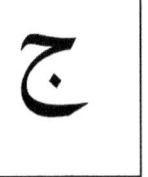

The Arabic letter is Jim, its number is 3 (which can be associated with spiritual authority). Its element is Water (desire for power), and the dot in the letter is in the middle of the world now, indicating the power struggles. It is said to be connected to patience, which seems to be very necessary here.

In the previous mansion the creative step was 'the Two Feet' referring to the entry in the second quarter of seven mansions, in which there is not only pure Mercy but also Wrath. Duality and struggle have arrived; it is not for nothing that these two mansions are associated with power. One of Al Terf's keywords is therefore Divine Wrath and its creative level is 'the Sphere without Stars', that is, the zodiac. Born with the Moon in this mansion you are very connected to this step in the creation process where all the potential is given; the zodiac is the highest sphere in which everything is contained. Leo wants it all and wants it now.

This mansion is all about confrontation with authority, adversity and frustration. In elections it is only good for battles and power struggles.

The malefic nature of this mansion does not mean it is all disaster; how the mansion works out exactly will be indicated by the context of the chart. However, the Leo themes will be present with the specific emphasis and tendency this mansion gives. It is instructive to compare this mansion with the next three - Al Jabba, Al Zubra and Al Sarfah - all of which are part of Leo. They will be described in the next three chapters. A good example of how Al Terf may work out in a life is the chart of George Michael, who had his Moon there; it illustrates that the delineation of the mansions should not be simplified by focusing on literal keywords.

George Michael was a hugely successful singer, although clearly there was a lot of frustration and misfortune in his life too. The first thing that we notice is the North Node on the ascendant. This is the Dragon's Head, the positive side of the life-energy axis that *wants* the world and also tends to *give* the world. It is a very Jupiter-like energy, at least as regards success, expansion and growth; it is definitely not good for spiritual development. The North Node on the ascendant inflates the ego, leaving little space for others on the descendant which automatically has the painful limiting South Node placed on it. This is not very helpful for relationships, as love is based on the sacrifice of the ego.

Benefic Jupiter is Lord 10 of the profession, indicating what happens in the public sphere and although it does not have any essential dignity, it is very strongly placed in the tenth house - Lord 10 in the tenth house is not bad for success. It is in sextile with a conjunction of Venus, the planet of the arts and Mercury the planet of voices, very strong in Gemini, one of the signs that has a 'voice'. Venus is not only the planet of the arts in a general sense, it is also Lord 5 of creativity. This conjunction is on powerful first magnitude star Rigel, a star in Orion the Hunter which tends to give a lot of success. On top of that royal Spica, also a star of great fame, is conjunct the fifth house cusp of creativity, and powerful first-magnitude Achernar is on the MC!

This is very favourable for achieving fame with musical talent. The position of the Venus-Mercury conjunction in the weak twelfth house is not a very big problem as the aspect with this very strong Jupiter, Lord 10 in the tenth house, frees Mercury-Venus from the twelfth house prison. Venus as Lord 5 is also the significator of sexuality and the conjunction with infertile shape-shifting Mercury is one of the traditional indicators for homosexuality, something George Michael kept hidden for a long time (12th house). Three planets in the twelfth house do indicate an extra sensitivity to addiction and to feelings of loneliness and depression. This is also the house of uncontrollable desires which harm us and for which we may be punished, therefore this is the house of prisons too (an addiction is a figurative prison). George has seen it all.

Interestingly, George Michael has Saturn, the planet of discipline and wisdom, very strong in its own sign as Lord 9 of spirituality on cusp 9 of

The 28 Mansions – Al Tarf

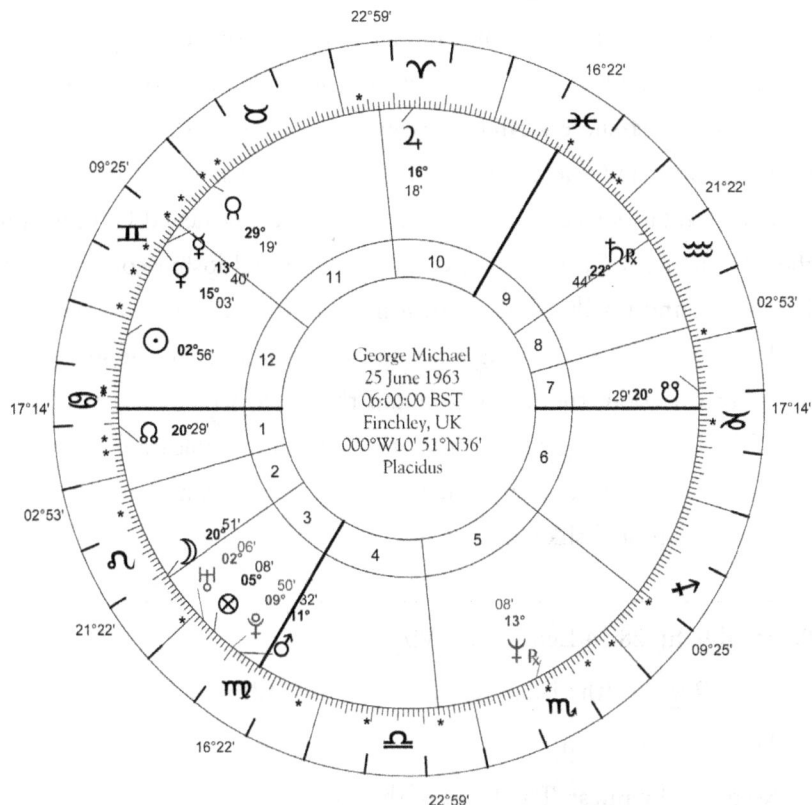

spiritual development! He could have saved himself from the self-destructive sex, drugs and rock'n roll life by becoming a traditional Catholic or a Buddhist monk for example; the potential is certainly there. Unfortunately the Moon is Lord 1, George Michael himself, and it is in opposition with Saturn, so he rejects it. The Moon/Lord 1 is placed in Leo and every planet in Leo hates Saturn because Leo is the sign where Saturn is in detriment; this is a negative reception. He hates his potential lifebuoy; he can see it floating around up there, but he does not want to grab it. What *does* he want? His Moon in Leo loves the Sun (fame) and his Part of the Moon in Virgo, representing his deepest hunger, wants its dispositor Mercury/Lord 12 in the twelfth house of all the things God has forbidden.

So with the North Node on the ascendant, powerful Achernar on the MC, Jupiter Lord 10 strong in the tenth house, royal Spica on the fifth house cusp and this Mercury/Venus conjunction on strong Rigel, the potential for mega-success can be clearly seen. Also with the strong twelfth house emphasis and the North Node on the ascendant the tendency to exceed all limitations can also be seen. This is strengthened by that same Achernar on the MC, with its myth of stealing and losing control of the solar chariot and finally coming down in flames. In all this Al Terf fits in fine. There is the all-consuming burning Leo ambition, and the success but also the provocation, the frustration and the misfortune. Of the rulers of Al Terf, Saturn is strong which shows that the more unpleasant tendencies of the mansion could have been controlled by this strong Saturn and its discipline which he dislikes so much.

---

10. Al Jabbah: 28.54 Leo – 11.45 Virgo

Star: Regulus (the Lion's Heart)/Al Jabbah/Adhafera

Arabic letter: Shin

Associated names: The Head of the Lion

Planets and energies: Mars-Jupiter – Rulership/success/royalty

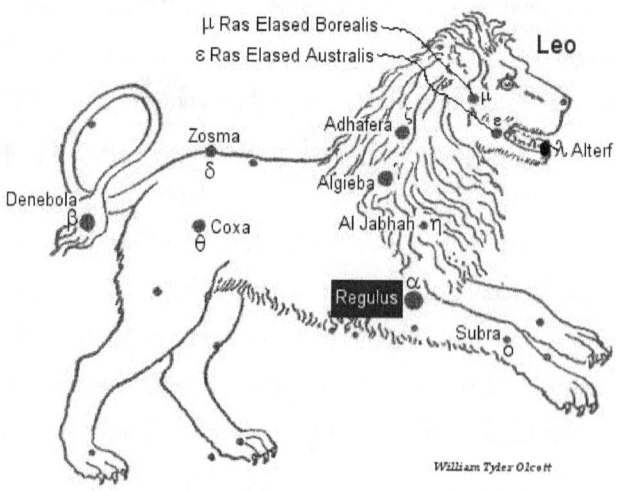

The 28 Mansions – Al Jabbah

The name of this tenth mansion Al Jabbah, means 'the Brow', the Lion's Brow. However, the most important descriptive star is mighty Regulus, the 'Little King' that 'leads to the throne'. It is the most royal star of the royals. On its own in a good position in the chart, it can make your career, especially if it is on the MC or the ascendant. Al Jabbah, the star that gives its name to this mansion, is much weaker than the bright and powerful Lion's Heart, Regulus, so this mansion could just as well have been named after Regulus as it brings all of its royal characteristics into play. Note that a Moon in Al Jabbah on its own is no guarantee for success, as always a mansion can only be judged in the context of the whole chart.

Al Jabbah is the second Leo mansion of which there are a total of four and each Leo mansion has another central star and another central part, so quite appropriately, Leo is big. They all share in the Nemean Lion story but each mansion brings a different emphasis and it is instructive to follow this 'line' of the stars going through the Leo constellation. In the previous mansion ruled by Al Terf, we confront the Lion as it spots us; the star Al Terf is on the outside, the first Leo star we meet coming from Cancer, but here in Al Jabbah we have arrived in the head and the heart, becoming part of its power, not confronting it any more. The third Leo mansion is ruled by Zosma on the back of the Lion, a position from which the Leo power can still be used very well. The central star in the fourth Leo mansion however is Denebola in the Tail, pointing to a loss of Leo power; this is the part where it is left behind.

Just by looking at the imagery you can grasp the meaning of a mansion, the differences between the mansions, and the line of development which would be indicated by the progressed Moon moving at the speed of about a mansion per year. Donald Trump's presidency can, for example, be followed by his progressed Moon moving through the mansions, and this will be discussed in the next chapters. The Leo myth will not be told again here, but it can be added that Leo also tends to bring stubbornness; it will continue even if it is clear that the battle is lost, and this may bring it down, so a fall from the throne is always a possibility.

The ruling planets here are Mars and Jupiter, quite appropriate for the Lion's Heart, and having arrived at the Heart and the Brow, the keywords are very positive. At the centre of the Lion its full potential is unleashed; great force, achievements, dominance and ascendancy, it's all about getting on the throne. The tenth mansion in the Vedic cycle is also connected to Regulus and has the same Leo connotations, to which can be added a pride in tradition and the glorious past.

The symbolic image is the impressive head of a lion, and its Arabic letter is Shin. It looks a bit like Leo, its element is Fire, its number is 300 (the 'spiritual' number 3 can be associated with authority), and it is said to be connected to personal destiny. The creative step is the sphere of the fixed stars; of the potential becoming visible in its effect.

This tenth Mansion is connected to success, strength, rulership and expansion, it is also good for love.

A good example of how this mansion may work out is the chart of Dolly Parton, no introduction required. Mercury, the planet of voices, is very important here as it rules the MC of the profession and the ascendant of the person. It is right on the cusp of the fifth house of creativity on the powerful first magnitude star Wega, the main star in the Lyre. The Lyre is also the Eagle coming down to earth where it will make known the beauty and wisdom it has seen in the heavens, and can therefore be associated with musicians and teachers. The Eagle is also sometimes seen as the Vulture; this more sinister side comes out more clearly in mundane astrology, but artistic activity and teaching are good keywords in the charts of people.

This very important Mercury on the creative fifth cusp – a cusp is a high-energy line where the house manifests most strongly – is in earthy

The 28 Mansions – Al Jabbah

Capricorn disposed by earthy Saturn. It is country music, not Beethoven and Bach. Saturn, planet of agriculture and Lord 5 of creativity, is retrograde and conjunct a rough retrograde Mars, meaning that intellectual avant-garde music is not the right description here either. This conjunction of Saturn/Lord 5 of creativity and Mars/Lord 3 of expression is found in the very positive eleventh house of the 'fruits of your labour' and it is on Pollux, the royal star of great success. Saturn is in its detriment and Mars in its fall, but fortunately these two have a lot of power to manifest as they are in a good house and on royal Pollux.

The measure of essential dignity of a planet only shows how effectively it is expressing its nature, it does not say too much about success. The whole context of the chart should be taken into account and weighed to evaluate this. It is very important in this process to make use of *all* the main techniques, many of which have been forgotten in modern astrology. To get a completely balanced picture of success we need to include the planetary parts and the synastry with the prenatal syzygy (Full Moon or New Moon) and eclipse charts.

A conjunction or opposition with one of the seven planetary parts will show a very intense, emphasized motive coming out in the life. A strong synastry of the radix with the prenatal syzygy (lunation) or eclipse chart indicates someone who is going to catch the spirit of the time in their personal activities, so there are very different ways in which people can become successful. It can be achieved by angular planets, an essentially strong planet, powerful fixed stars, a good lunar mansion, prenatal synastry, planet parts or most often a combination of these factors.

In Dolly Parton's chart the Part of Saturn and the Part of Mars are conjunct her Saturn (Lord 5)/Mars (Lord 3) by antiscion (position mirrored in the 0° Cancer/0° Capricorn polarity axis). This conjunction of Saturn/Mars is much emphasized as it is repeated by the planetary parts in conjunction with it! This gives a special motive not only psychologically but also in a tangible way, as this is an aspect with a natal position through

The Lunar Mansions Guide

which the things connected to the parts happen as events and situations. What could be more country than the essences of Mars and Saturn? It is enlightening to note that these parts move extremely fast, as a few minutes later they are out of orb - the chart of a baby born five minutes later would not have this conjunction. So this is very personal for Dolly Parton; in this way differences can be seen even in charts of twins born right after each other.

Also her synastry with the prenatal eclipse chart is very strong; the artistic planet Venus is on the ascendant of this prenatal eclipse chart, Jupiter is on the MC on royal Spica and her natal chart picks up these strong positions. She will be able to ride the wave of the spirit of the times. In addition, Venus in the fifth house in the natal chart has its contribution to make to her fame; it is on Terebellum, one of the stars of fate, and

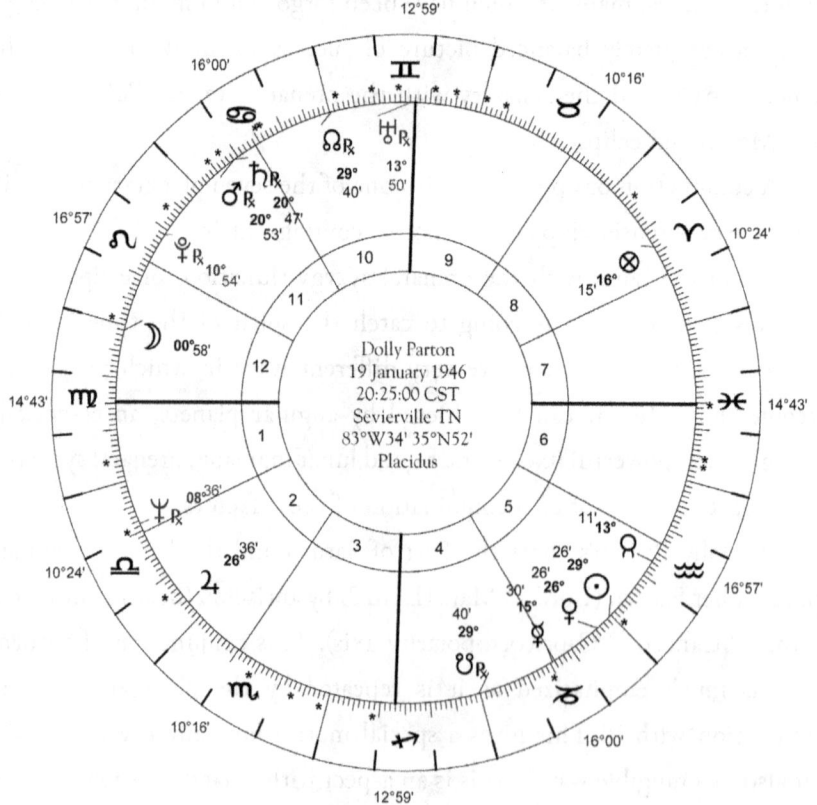

Venus will have a decisive influence in the life. This significator of love and women sees the Sun, significator of men, disappearing into the next sign. It reflects one of her most famous songs 'I will always love you' which is about splitting up, also shown by Venus' dispositor Saturn who wants to hold on but is in detriment, so it can't.

Last but not least, Uranus on the MC stands out. Uranus is the ultimate theme of coming down to earth. It is the primordial sky god castrated by Saturn, so yes, country again. Naturally Jupiter cannot be forgotten, as with the planet of expansion on royal Spica in the second house of money squaring Venus as described above, she is going to make some money. It is an immensely strong chart despite the fact that there is no planet with any decent essential dignity in it. Powerful Al Jabbah, the Lion's Head, fits in very nicely, and its rulers are Jupiter and Mars. Need I say more?

---

11. **Al Zubrah:** 11.45 Virgo – 24.36 Virgo

   Star: Maagd – Zosma/Coxa (the Lion's Back)

   Arabic letter: Ya

   Associated names: The Lion's Brow/The Lion's Rider

   Planets and energies: Saturn/Venus – Profits/rulership/success

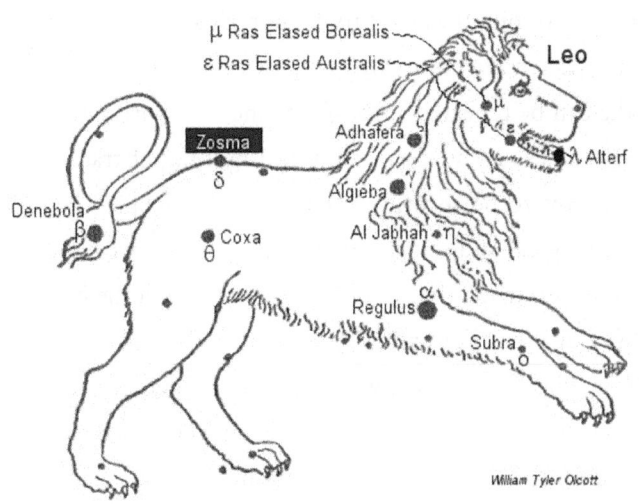

In the introduction to the mansions in Part 1 it was explained that the knowledge of this ancient system has become obsolete and that there is a lot of confusion about it. As it was seldom used in other than a rather crude way, irregularities tend to pop up so it's necessary to spend some time figuring it out. The name of this mansion is a case in point; it is called Al Zubra, Arabic for 'the Mane' (of the Lion), however, its most important descriptive star, Zosma, is clearly not in the Mane, it is on the back - so a more appropriate name for the mansion would be 'the Back'. To make things even more complicated there is a star called Subra on the lower leg of Leo! So what is going on here?

It is clear from the information about the mansion that this is all about the Back. This is confirmed by the line of ruling stars described in the previous chapter, indicating the consecutive parts of Leo connected to the four Leo mansions. The Eyes come first (Alterf), then the Heart and the Head (Regulus and Al Jabbah, see the picture overleaf), in which the Mane could be included and then as third and fourth mansions the Back (Zosma) and the Tail (Denebola). This is logical and consistent, so the conclusion can be drawn that the name of the mansion is wrong as it does not refer to the part of Leo under discussion.

The simple reason for this confusion may be linguistic, as the back is 'Al Zuhr' in Arabic. It is easy to change this into Al Zubra; authors of traditional texts tend to copy things uncritically out of respect for the past, so a mistake can be repeated throughout the ages without anyone noticing the inconsistencies. To have a good understanding of traditional astrology all methods have to be scrutinized, and not just copied because they are old. Are they logical and, most importantly, do they work in practice? The truth is not necessarily given in old texts, so it would be better to call this mansion Al Zuhr, but I am afraid this would only add more confusion. So it is Al Zuhr, 'the Back', but it will not be re-named as such.

As this is still the middle part of the Lion all the Leo themes apply here - and they seem to come to full flowering in this phase. The mythological

The 28 Mansions – Al Zubrah

story of the Nemean Lion is relevant with all its associations, and the Back is certainly a position of strength so the keywords are very positive; it is about power acquired, authority, high position, royalty and appeal. The ruling planets are Saturn and Venus, indicating a mixture of tough staying-power and attraction.

The symbolic image is very clear as it confirms this meaning very strongly. It is a powerful warrior heavily armed and riding on the back of the lion, its power fully deployed. The Arabic letter is Ya, its number is 10, the number of full manifestation in the world, its element is Air and most appropriately it is associated with God's help.

The creative step is 'the first Sky' or Sphere of Saturn, the highest planet, the first very specific manifestation of the divine potential (though it does not indicate a specific Saturnian nature of this mansion). The Vedic system has three Leo mansions: its eleventh mansion is also ruled by Zosma, and its themes are more or less the same although marriage, sex and love are more emphasized. These corresponding Vedic themes may function as suggestions to extend the meanings of the mansion if this makes sense, as it seems to do in this case.

This eleventh mansion is about power, winning, rulership and royalty.

The chart example is a progression of the Moon through the mansions in Donald Trump's chart when he lost the presidency in November 2020. It can be seen (by moving the progressions backward) how much stronger his progressions were four years before in 2016 at the time of his election (discussed above), with his progressed Sun on mighty Regulus (yes, the throne) placed on his natal ascendant and his ascendant moving over the progressed Great Benefic Jupiter on royal Spica. The progressed Moon was then moving into Al Dhira which is a mansion strongly connected with

The Lunar Mansions Guide

success, and Mercury the ruler of Al Dhira is strong in his natal chart. But now these very strong and favourable positions have been left far behind. It is helpful that with progressions (directions for the angles), you can clearly see this continuous flow of developments and the changes of the tide.

His loss was predicted publicly by me about a year before the election in 2020, on the basis of the progressions and the very unfavourable lunar return of the election month. This lunar return had the South Node, indicating a painful sacrifice, with the Moon (popular support) on the ascendant (Trump that month). That did not look like a re-election and this judgement was confirmed by the progressions/directions in November 2020. As explained above for the main line of development six factors are checked: the slow progressed/directed Sun, Ascendant and MC and the

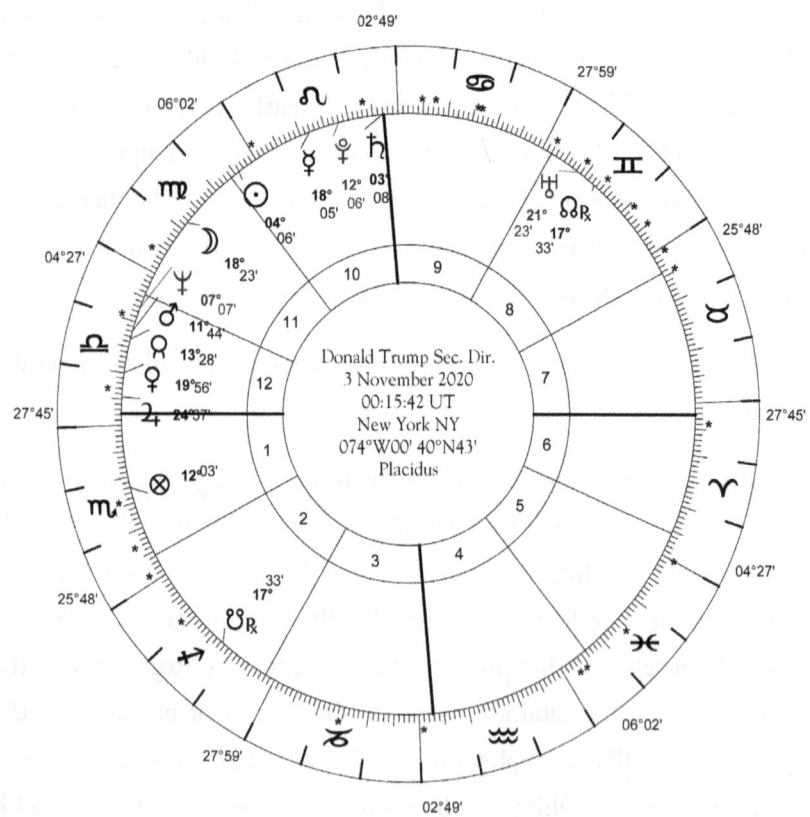

much faster progressed/directed Moon, the Part of the Moon (Part of Fortune) and the Part of the Sun. So this amounts to the angles, the Luminaries and the Parts of the Luminaries, to which will be added anything else that stands out in the chart.

The first clear sign of his loss of the 2020 elections in these progressions is the MC conjunct the progressed Saturn. As Saturn moves very slowly its progressed position can always safely be ignored in prediction, unless it is activated by a faster factor as in this case. It is the MC that brings Saturn to life and makes its detriment in Leo relevant, where the Great Malefic will show its nastiest sides. That looks like a big disappointment. The Part of the Sun is conjunct the progressed Mars, the other malefic, also in its detriment so this is not very nice at all. On top of that, this conjunction is on the nasty star Vindemiatrix, connected to falling, premature harvesting and an arrogant overestimation of one's powers - so disappointment again. It should be noted that the Part of the Sun moves backward through the signs because of its formula.

The Part of Fortune (Part of the Moon) is almost on the South Scale, a very powerful malefic star of justice, on which you have to pay dearly for what you have done; it is Scorpio's Claw of revenge. The progressed position of the Moon by antiscion opposes the progressed Part of the Sun conjunct Mars on Vindemiatrix, giving it a very strong emphasis. So the Part of the Sun, that is the essence of the Sun – the king - and the Moon (his people), are separating with a very nasty Mars – the planet of quarrels – directly involved. The further we look, the more problems pop up.

Two important things should be noted: these three factors move fast, at one degree a month, making them really quite precise in timing. We don't have to stick to a very strict orb of one degree as it may be a bit more, but because of this high speed, it will take us close to the month that something happens. An analysis of the lunar returns will provide certainty about the month. The second important thing is that although a progressed chart is often spoken of, there is no such thing, and actually this is very confusing. Progressed positions are no more than *calculated* positions, so although the result looks like a chart, it is not a chart and it should not be delineated as such. Progressed houses do not exist!

Now that the standard progressions and directions have been checked and a clear idea established of what will happen, the lunar mansion the Moon is moving through can be investigated. It is a good idea not to start with this but to end with it, to make sure it will be delineated in context. As discussed previously, when Trump won the presidency in November 2016 his progressed Moon was entering successful Al Dhira. Three years later, in September 2019 there was a progressed New Moon, always a moment of crisis, and then the first impeachment procedure started. At the same time the Moon was entering Al Jabbah, the powerful Regulus mansion, an indication that the procedure would not succeed. In May 2020 the progressed Moon entered Al Zubra and six months of intense campaigning started. This is the Zosma mansion, and he is the warrior on the lion.

That does not look bad, although one of the planetary rulers of the mansion, Saturn, is very weak in his natal chart, in its detriment and conjunct the other planetary ruler, Venus, which is Lord 10 of the profession. However, it is the change of mansion the Moon is approaching that is decisive. In early 2021 (the official moment his presidency ended) it left powerful Al Zubra to enter the fourth Leo mansion Al Sarfah, the Lion's Tail. During the campaign Trump was still on the lion in Al Zubra and he indeed did do very well as many Americans voted for him. However, in Al Sarfah the warrior is on foot, the Tail is the end of Leo, so he has stepped down. Within the context of the other progressions and the knowledge of what is happening, this could only mean he would lose.

The 28 Mansions – Al Sarfah

12. Al Sarfah: 24.36 Virgo – 7.28 Libra

Star: Denebola (the Lion's Tail)

Arabic letter: Dad

Associated names: The Changer/The Dragon Slayer

Planets and energies: Saturn/Venus - Fighting/conflict/discord

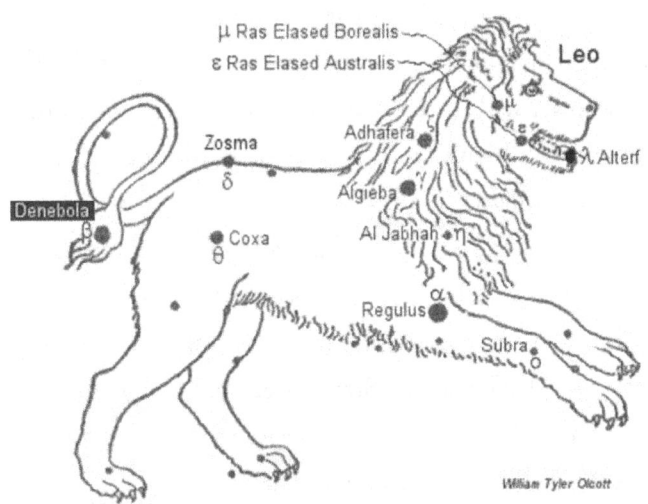

The twelfth mansion is the last of the four Leo mansions, and this is the Tail, the last part of Leo. Its name Al Sarfah in Arabic means 'the Changer' and indeed in this part of the Leo series things are about to change. Leo will soon be left behind and the preparation for it is in the Tail. In Al Terf the Leo power was confronted, in Al Jabba – the Head - and Al Zubra - the Back, it was used and in Al Sarfah it is left behind, but in Leo this is not going happen without a painful struggle. The example chart in the chapter on Al Zubra showed Donald Trump's progressed Moon changing mansions when he lost the election, from Al Zubra (riding on The Back of the Lion) to Al Sarfah (falling off the Back in the part associated with the Tail).

It is all Leo energy so there will be a fierce power struggle and one of Leo's mythical characteristics is its perseverance; it will go on even when it would unquestionably be wiser to stop. Remember this is the Nemean lion, the symbol of an extreme lust for power and a burning ambition; it wants to be number one at all costs and will fight on until it cannot go on any longer. The refusal of Donald Trump to admit his loss in the 2020 elections and to congratulate his opponent is typical for Leo. He tried everything to stop Joe Biden from being inaugurated and in the end he was not present when it happened. Leo may be royal but it is not always generous in defeat, as it wants to win at all costs.

So it can be imagined that when Leo is left behind there is a problem; letting go of power will not be a smooth process. The keywords associated with this mansion all have to do with clashes, loss of position, quarrels and expulsion. This is mirrored in the planets ruling this part of Leo - Saturn of limitation and sacrifice, and Venus of connection and love. The same planets ruled Al Zubra, but this is another part of Leo so they will have another effect, and these descriptions of the planets are quite general. Its ruling star is Denebola, the Tail Star in Leo, and it is often associated with the provocation of the rulers, very appropriate for this place, which is not part of the Leo main body any more.

The symbolic image is very clear. It is a warrior on foot, fighting a fierce dragon; he does not ride the Lion any more. The Arabic letter is Dad, which, quite amazingly seems to be a graphical picture of the tail. Its number is 800, a doubled 4 of tensions, multiplied by 100; its element is Air, pointing to the movement here, and its theme is to disclose tensions, which have resulted in open battle. The creative step is the second planet sphere of Jupiter, also called 'He who knows'. Note this does not mean this mansion is like Jupiter, it is the position in the creative cycle that matters; the creative impulse is descending through the planetary spheres, giving out the specific energies the cosmos is composed of. In the Vedic system the twelfth mansion is also ruled by Denebola, with the usual Leo themes, love and sexuality being added as extra themes in the Vedic descriptions.

The 28 Mansions – Al Sarfah

This mansion is all about battle, conflict, power struggles and confrontation.

A good example of how this mansion may work out is the chart of Meghan Markle, the American actress who married Prince Harry of Windsor. The couple decided, after having fulfilled royal duties for some years, to break with the royal family; they left for the US to have a life of their own. Here it can be seen how important it is to have a mansion in the background, steering life-changing decisions like this one, which for Meghan was certainly one of the most dramatic she would ever take. As mentioned previously Prince Harry has Al Botein as his lunar mansion, the second Aries mansion, which is very fiery and connected to confrontations, so that is quite a combination with Al Sarfah!

In Meghan's chart we immediately notice the three-fold conjunction of the Moon, Saturn and Jupiter in Libra close to the IC. The Moon is Lord 1, showing Meghan Markle 'in her life' and it is very closely conjunct Saturn Lord 7 of relationship, and Jupiter Lord 9 of foreign countries is the general significator of aristocracy. Such a tight three-fold conjunction, including Lord 1 will emphasize the associated themes very strongly, which is extra-highlighted by the Part of Venus at 8.27 Aries opposing Jupiter. A planetary part in conjunction or opposition with a natal factor within a two-degree orb indicates a very specific individual theme in the life, so the essence of love the part symbolises is connected very specifically for her to this three-fold conjunction.

The opposition shows the tensions this will bring. One of the other parts, the Part of the Moon (Fortuna) is on the MC by antiscion, illustrating she will fullfill an essentially lunar function in the public arena. It is clear, she is 'the wife of' and 'the mother of' his (ex-)royal children; an antiscion is a shadow point which quite nicely indicates the nature of this role. Her husband is not the crown prince, but 'in his shadow', and she is the shadow's wife. So these parts do not only show intense motivations, but also actual situations in life if they are much emphasized, as in this case.

The ascendant is in the middle of two very powerful stars. It is close to royal Pollux and to mighty Procyon, but it is not easy to decide which star has the most influence. Pollux is a bit closer in latitude, Procyon a bit closer in longitude. Both stars would fit well, however, as Pollux is a royal success star and Procyon is the main star in the smart Small Dog that defies the powers that be and does it all its own way. On the other side on the descendant is Terebellum, one of the three stars of fate, indicating that the marriage will be a fateful event in Meghan's life, an event with very important consequences. The Part of Marriage is on the descendant by antiscion, emphasizing the marriage theme even more.

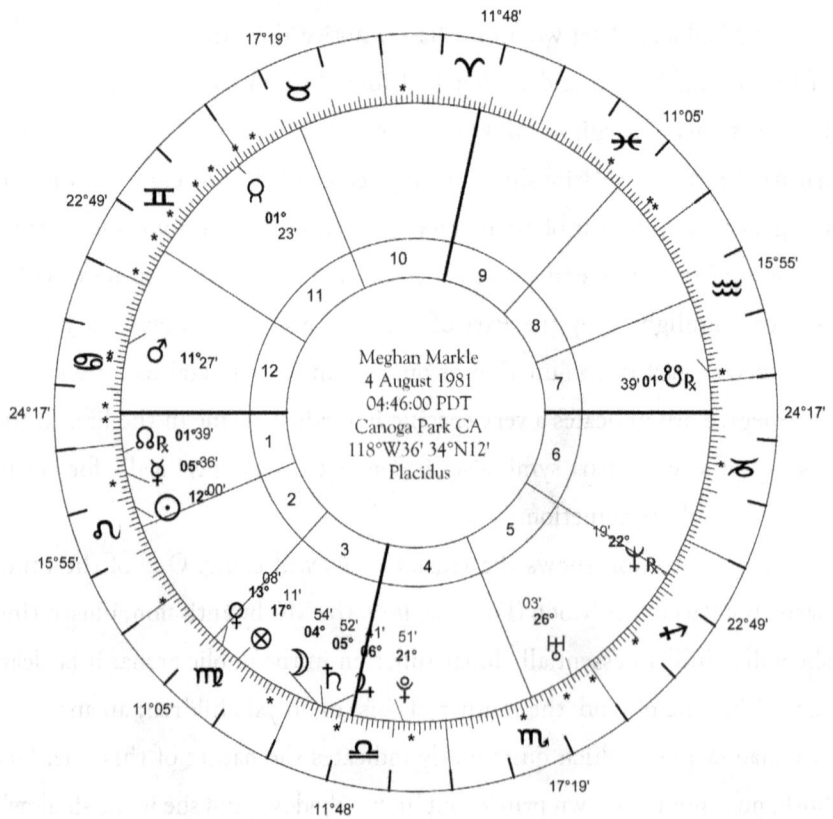

In the first house, Mercury is placed on chaotic Praesepe, the Empty Crib much associated with splitting up. Mercury is Lord 12 of self-destruction and uncontrollable impulses, not a very nice combination as Praesepe has no guiding principle, and neither has shape-shifting pragmatic Mercury, whose power of manifestation is strengthened further by the conjunction with the North Node. Mars is Lord 10 of the profession is on powerful Sirius, the main star of the Big Dog in a narrow sextile with Venus, the planet of art, providing a way out of the weak twelfth house for Mars/Lord 5 of creativity, and showing the acting career. All in all, there is a lot of power to be seen here. These two bright stars on the ascendant, the royal Sun in Leo, Mercury on the North Node in the first house... This three-fold conjunction and the Parts of the Moon and Venus are very much involved.

However, the problems are also clear. Fierce Procyon defies the powers that be, Mercury in the first house on the expansive North Node on 'splitting-up' Praesepe is uncontrollable Lord 12, the fate star Terebellum is in on the descendant of relationship and the Part of Venus opposes the aristocratic marriage conjunction. So in this context Al Sarfah will strengthen the conflict, the battle with the Lion and the tendency to provoke, irritate and fight the ruler. A woman with her Moon in Al Sarfah marrying into a royal family is bad news. The planetary ruler Venus is essentially weak in its fall, Saturn is strong in exaltation, so it is half strong, half weak. Yes she did marry him, and she did not shy away from the duties of Saturn immediately and was part of it all for some time, but in the end her weak Venus could not take it any more. So the warrior decided to get off the Lion and to fight the royal beast on foot.

The Lunar Mansions Guide

13. Al Awwa: 7.28 Libra – 20.19 Libra

Star: Zavijava (Virgo's Breast and Wings)

Arabic letter: Lam

Associated names: The Wings/The Lovers

Planets and energies: Mercury/Mars – Love/union/sexuality

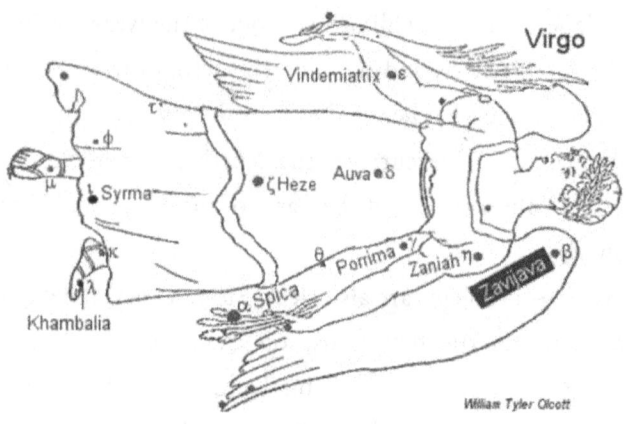

In this thirteenth mansion the Leo constellation, strongly associated with power struggles and authority, is left behind and a whole different energy zone starts in Virgo. Virgo does not have anything to do with power; its story is associated with purification. It is about sorting out what is worth keeping and rejecting everything that is too earthly to enable the soul to receive the spirit. Obviously in Christianity it is Mary, the Holy Mother of God, who receives the spirit because she was conceived without sin. In ancient mythology Virgo is Astraea, a daughter of Titans - the Earth giants representing material bondage - who chooses the side of the gods (the divine) against her Titanic family roots.

It is clear that this is a Virgo mansion but there is a strange anomaly here requiring some attention. The descriptive star is said to be Zavijava, but the problem is that Zavijava's tropical position was 27.20 Virgo in the year 2000. This means that the distance to the boundary of Al Awwa is

The 28 Mansions – Al Awwa

10 degrees, almost a complete lunar mansion, so obviously this cannot be correct. Although a descriptive star does not have to be right on the boundary, it should at least be close to it. The basic problem is that we are combining a systematic division by 28 with irregular constellations and this will not fit perfectly.

This mansion may be seen as the Wings of Virgo but Zavijava cannot be taken as its star. Zaniah or Caphir would be more appropriate, as stars placed also on the wings or the arms seem to boil down to the same meaning. So the translation of Al Awwa, 'the Wings' can be kept, but Zavijava as its determining star is illogical. This may seem to be an argument to use mansions of different lengths, but that system has other disadvantages. It has to be accepted that when working in a lunar mode imperfection tends to pop up, but of course gross irregularities like this one have to be corrected.

So the name 'the Wings' – Al Awwa – can be kept and it is clear what meaning it gives to this mansion. The central issue in the Virgin is of pure earth receiving spirit; alchemically it is the union of male Sulphur with female Mercury, which can only take place after the purification of Mercury by distillation. In practical plant alchemy this means you distill the plant alcohol carrying the Mercury principle to get rid of the water, which represents earthly desires. It is the same process here, a union of masculine and feminine is effected, the wings indicating a connection with 'above' (distillation is also going up) which is where the masculine spirit comes from. It is only logical that this mansion is associated with the connection of the sexes, with love, attraction and sexuality. The Wings have as their planetary rulers Mars, sexual energy and Mercury, connection. Sex should not be seen here only as action between the sheets but also as a creative, complementary polarity between masculine and feminine energies in a wider sense.

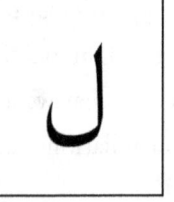 The symbolic image does not beat around the bush; it is a naked man sexually desiring a woman. Its letter is Lam, its number is 30, so 3 symbolising the union of the two poles multiplied by 10, totally manifested in the world. Its element is Earth, the real physical union, and is said to refer, quite appropriately, to the connection to the Source of Union. The form of the letter seems to indicate this meaning of the connection of the earth with the divine creative energy coming down from above.

The creative step is the sphere of Mars, and called 'the Victorious', it reflects the vital energy becoming earthly. In the planetary symbol of Mars, the circle of the divine energy is placed *under* the cross of matter. Again it does not mean this mansion is very martial in a more realistic or literal way, it only shows where in the cycle this mansion stands; it is a description of its nature in a more theoretical sense.

In this mansion it is all about love, attraction, charm, connection and sexuality.

A good example of how this mansion may work out is the chart of Leonardo DiCaprio. The guideline is to delineate the natal chart first and then look at the lunar mansion, but in this case the lunar mansion seems to say it all very clearly - Di Caprio started his career as a sex symbol and this is what Al Awwa is all about. The planetary rulers of the Wings, Mars and Mercury, have some essential and accidental dignity in his chart, so he will be able to manifest the promise of the mansion in an effective way. This Mars is very important in his chart, very strong in its domicile and disposing two other planets. It is also in trine with the Great Benefic Jupiter in its domicile and placed in the second house of money. So by using the Mars energy, the general significator of masculinity, he will also be able to earn quite a lot of money.

There are no very powerful fixed stars on important places in the chart but there are other ways to be successful. The planetary part of

The 28 Mansions – Al Awwa

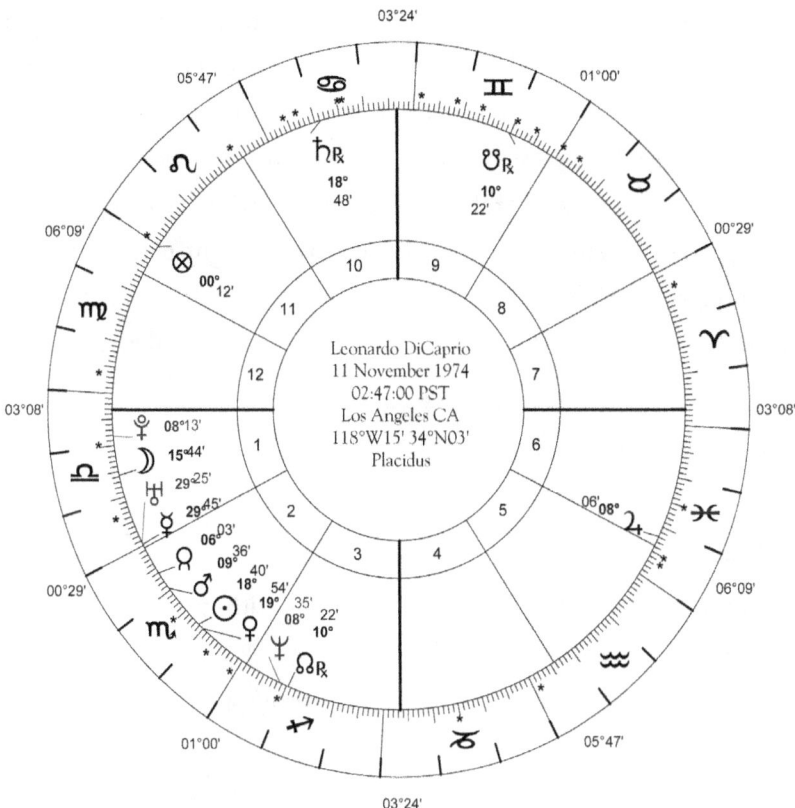

Jupiter, the Part of Victory for example, is on the fifth house cusp of creativity and the Venus Part of Love is on the expansive North Node on royal Antares. Lord 5 of creativity is retrograde Saturn in its detriment but it will be able to manifest strongly as it is placed in the tenth house of the profession. Saturn is in very strong reception with the Moon, Lord 10 of the profession, which itself is in the first house; this is a very powerful reception connecting the first house (the person) and the tenth house (the profession). The Moon is in the sign where Saturn has its exaltation and Saturn is in the sign ruled by the Moon.

This retrograde Saturn in a Water sign and its detriment is a graphic description of how he became famous, by the movie photo of the Titanic sticking up into the air just before sinking. This is one of those moments for astro-shivers as Saturn is by antiscion conjunct the South Node (going down) right on the Part of Fame! This gives a good idea of how even an essentially very weak planet can make your career. Had it been tucked away in the twelfth house it would not have become visible but in the tenth house visibility is no problem. The synastry with the prenatal eclipse and syzygy is also strong, showing he will be the right person to do the right thing at the right time and in the right place. This prenatal synastry enables you to catch the spirit of the times in your personal activities.

---

14. Al Simak: 20.19 Libra – 3.10 Scorpio

Star: Spica (Virgo's Wheat Ear)

Arabic letter: Nun

Associated names: The Unarmed/The Dog with its tail in its mouth

Planets and energies: Venus/Mars – Divorce/splitting up/separation

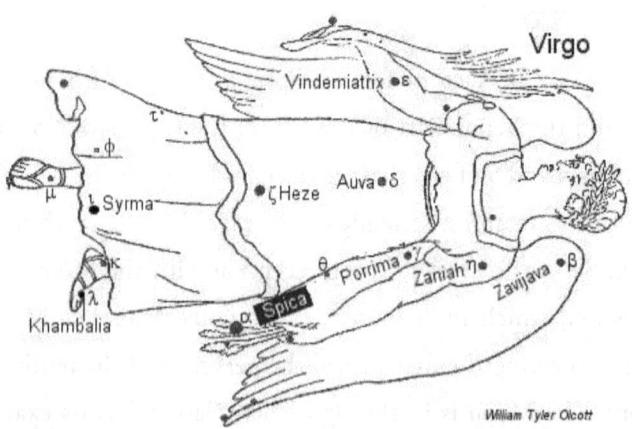

The fourteenth mansion is called Al Simak which is Arabic for 'the Unarmed', and it refers to the nature of Virgo. Virgo is the constellation of harvesting and purifying in order to be able to contact higher dimensions, to receive the spirit. The atmosphere is totally different from what was

seen in the previous constellation of Leo, where a power struggle was of the essence. There is no such thing here, no fighting, no weapons, and although there is a struggle, it has a totally different nature. This is the second of the three Virgo mansions, and the descriptive star is Spica, the Wheat Ear, which is the concentration point of the Virgoan harvesting process.

As explained previously this process is connected to the relationship between the earthly feminine and the spiritual masculine principles. So this mansion too can be associated with love and relationships, but as we have moved from the wings of Virgo to the Ear, the whole harvesting process has reached another stage. The wings in Al Awwa referred to 'above', to the first, idealistic impulse but the Sheaf is the phase in which things are finally sorted out; some things will be rejected, others will be kept. This is a less enthusiastic mansion, so the relationships indicated here have to go through a reality check, and there is more potential for friction.

This is reflected in the planetary rulers of this part of the Virgo constellation; Venus for love and Mars for fighting. The descriptive star Spica is seen as a very fortunate star as it gives, as it were, the full benefits of the harvesting - that is why it is always said it will take you further than you could ever have imagined. Lady Diana Spencer had Spica on her MC, and this gives a clear idea of what the constellation can bring. The whole 'Queen of Hearts' charisma certainly fits in with the Virgo purification process. Such a position does not mean everything is going to be all right, but Spica on the MC is certainly a powerful boost for the career. In the Vedic system Spica has a very special role to play as it marks the beginning of the sidereal zodiac at the point opposing itself. This gives the whole sidereal zodiac the sense of being a struggle for purification.

So this mansion can, like the previous one, be associated with love and relationships but there are more problems here. Its traditional keywords reflect this: splitting up, distancing, divorce, partition. This seems to give the mansion too negative a flavour, as it cannot be compared to the two first fiery Aries mansions for example, and there is also the favourable influence of Spica here, which is good for success. It does show, and this is the value of the mansions in the delineation of the chart, the process going on and this process will work out better if it is done consciously, if the most positive role in the myth connected to the constellation is chosen and lived out purposefully.

The symbolic image in this mansion is a dog holding its tail in its mouth which seems a bit mysterious. However, biting your own tail is a very well-known alchemical symbol; it refers to the Ouroboros, the dragon biting its own tail. It indicates exactly this Virgoan purification process, a circle of again and again going through the same work of sorting out, rejecting that which is impure and keeping that which has proven its value. It is a picture of the alchemical distillation cycle by which the Mercury, the soul in alchemy, is purified.

The Arabic letter is Nun; its element is Air, referring to purification of earthly things. Its number 25, which is 5 times 5 referring to the fifth 'high' element of Ether above the 4 more earthly elements and controlling them. Nun is the abbreviation of Ramadan, the month of fasting, a process of purification in order to connect to the higher dimensions. The letter is a rather precise picture of what is going on here, the half-circle symbolising the world below and the dot indicating the higher regions to be connected to. It is said to be an intermediary between principle and manifestation, exactly what Virgo is all about. The world was originally a full circle but as can be seen here, it was broken by sin, by the separation from God and purification is required to become reconnected; this is also the immaculate conception of Mary so clearly associated with the Virgo constellation. The step in the creative process is 'the planet sphere' or the 'sky' of the Sun, the visible symbol of God in our world; it is also called the

Light. In the Vedic system the connection with realities behind material appearances is also much emphasised, so again, the same basic theme.

This fourteenth mansion is all about relationships accompanied by frictions, connecting or letting go, severance, critically sorting out that which can lead to success.

A good example of how this may work out in a life is the chart of former French president François Mitterand. One of the most striking characteristics in his long career was his ability to adapt and change at the right moment. This can be seen immediately in his first house, representing most directly Mitterand himself. Planets in this house will greatly influence the life, as this house is the individual and in it the most fluid planets are found; pragmatic shape-shifter Mercury and the ever-changing Moon lacking fixed structure. So his ability to adapt to changing circumstances is anchored in his basic psychological make-up, given by these planets in the first house.

The Moon is Lord 10, the ruler of the profession and so it comes to him almost automatically. This Moon is also on Spica, this very favourable royal star. The Moon is not only on Spica but also in the mansion connected to the Wheat Ear. These two functions of the Moon, as a Luminary, as one of the seven planets on a star and as the indicator of the phase in the creative process, 'the step' in the mansion cycle, should be clearly distinguished from each other. It is possible that the Moon is placed on a star which does not describe the mansion the Moon is in, but this is not the case here, so everything is clear. The whole idea of a great career is further strengthened by mighty Pluto on the MC, and the Lord of the Underworld is able to strike overwhelmingly at the right moment.

Mercury in the first house is in the sign of Libra, ruled by Venus, and Venus is Lord 1 in Virgo ruled by Mercury, so Mercury and Venus are strongly connected by mutual reception. Mercury is Lord 12 of hidden things, Venus Lord 1 is placed in the twelfth house, so Mitterand has a natural affinity with what goes on behind the scenes, very necessary for a politician. It also seems to refer to the fact that he had a life-long mistress with whom he even had a daughter, which apparently didn't seem to affect his marriage too much. His Part of Fortune (or Part of the Moon), his hunger, is in the twelfth house disposed by Mercury and the other Part of a Luminary, the Part of the Sun is in the first house, disposed by Venus in this mutual reception with Mercury. Wherever you look there's a very strong emphasis on the twelfth house of secrecy. It comes as no surprise that one of his nicknames was the Sphinx, because it was never totally clear to others what he was up to.

The antiscion positions of the Parts of the Sun and the Moon are also interesting. The placement of a planetary part in a sign or a house only

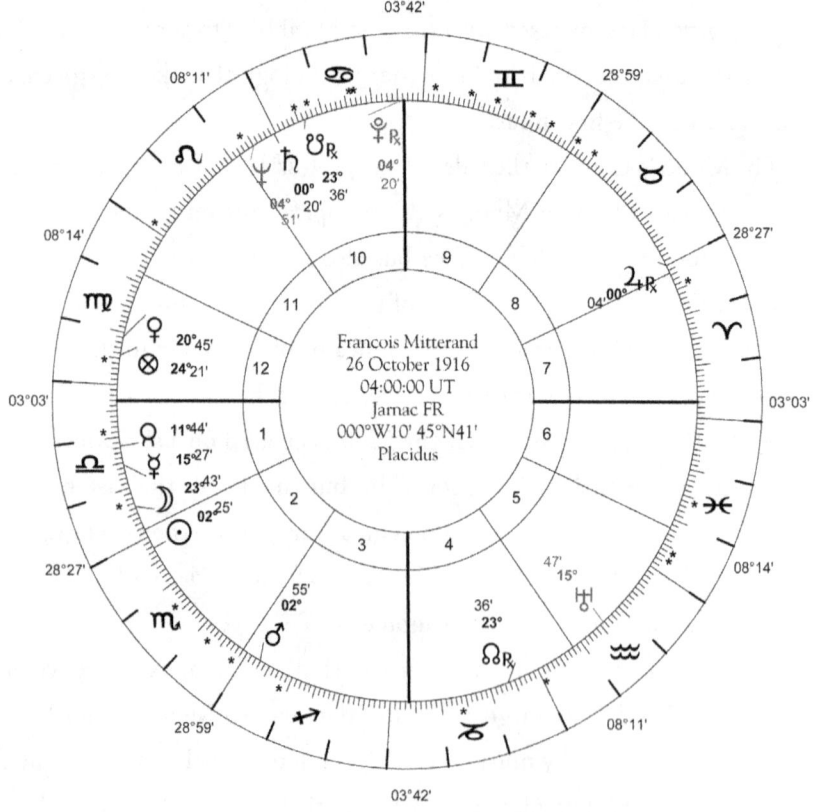

shows a 'psychological' tendency, so the Part of the Sun in the first house disposed by Lord 1 (Mitterand) indicates the tendency to see the future (the Part of the Sun essentially shows where we feel the connection to God, our only future) in himself, in his own actions and initiatives. A conjunction or opposition (2° orb) of the Part with an astrological factor like a planet or a cusp however, shows a real event or situation. By antiscion the Part of the Sun opposes Lord 1, so he will, with some friction, connect with the solar essence (the presidency). The antiscion of the Part of the Moon is on the descendant of relationships; the Part of Fortune is the lunar part, whereas an antiscion is hidden. It all indicates a hunger for others, but also connected to something indirect or hidden (antiscion) in relationships (descendant) and with women (Moon) - the mistress again.

Al Simak fits in seamlessly with this adaptive behaviour of Virgo, continually weighing everything and letting go of what is not of value any more. It is the harvesting; what can I keep that would further my position? Also the whole Virgo relationship theme is very clear in his life; he remained married all his life but had a mistress with whom he had a daughter. The planetary rulers Venus and Mars can be seen at work here - love with problems. Venus is in fall and Mars peregrine in his chart; the less essential dignity the rulers have, the stronger the less pleasant tendencies in the mansion will manifest.

Third Quarter of Seven Mansions

15. Al Ghafr: 3.10 Scorpio – 16.02 Scorpio

    Star: Syrma (Virgo's robe)

    Arabic letter: Ra

    Associated names: The Covering/The Robe/The Scribe

    Planets and energies: Mercury/Mars – Profits/business success

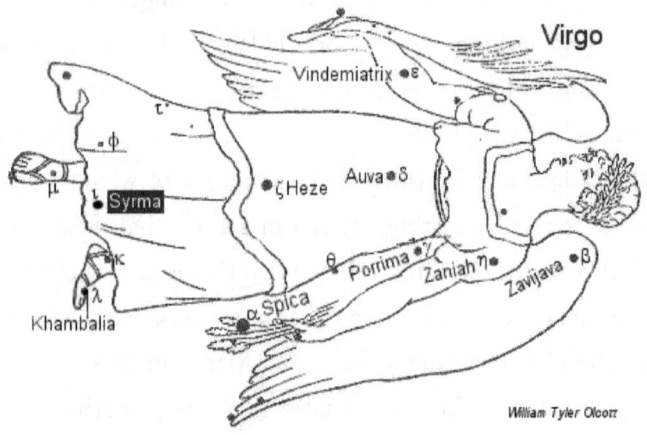

William Tyler Olcott

This mansion is the third and last of the three Virgo mansions, and also the start of the third quarter of the creative cycle. This is the halfway point, corresponding in the archetypical picture of the cycle overlaid on the tropical zodiac to the autumn equinox, opposite the beginning in Aries. The name Al Ghafr is Arabic for 'the Covering' and the picture above clearly shows why. The zone in the constellation entered here is, after the Wings and the Sheaf, the Robe near the feet, so again the focus is changing, the whole purification process is becoming more earthly, connected as it is with the feet and the robe pointing to more outward things. It is important to understand that the 28 mansions are 28 'constellational zones' with a specific nature through which the Moon is moving.

The 28 Mansions – Al Ghafr

It is still the mythology of Virgo that applies here, so the whole idea of carefully sorting out what is useful will manifest through this mansion. The question may come up why on earth Syrma, and another one nearby, Kappa Virginis, are mentioned as the descriptive stars of this mansion. These stars are not found in any list of stars relevant and effective in astrology as is another star nearby on the foot, Khambalia, so why not take Khambalia? Also Syrma is not very bright, so what is the reason for the apparently strange role it is playing here? The answer is that Syrma is on Virgo's Robe and that is the central point in this mansion.

The descriptive star has to express the essential nature of the constellational zone and its symbolism represented by the mansion, so it has to reflect the special focus. This shows it is not about only stars here, it is also about constellations - groups of stars, or more exactly parts of constellations of some specific nature. This nature here is 'the Covering' or the Robe, and this more outward nature combined with the selection process of Virgo leads to the keywords given for this mansion; it all has do with business and financial success. This is certainly not the only mansion related to success, but its specific nature shows in every case *how* this is earned. There are many ways to succeed, and for every person this is different; that is why there are no general recipes or techniques to achieve success.

One of the planets associated with this mansion is very appropriately Mercury, the planet of trade and business, the energy of figures and attention for details. Mars is the other planet describing this mansion showing decisive action in business. The symbolic image of a man holding scrolls and writing letters reflects this nature.

The associated letter is Ra, its element is most appropriately Earth, its number 200 (earthly duality multiplied into total manifestation), and it is said to symbolise a message, which all seems to point to

The Lunar Mansions Guide

the Mercurial nature of this mansion. In the Vedic system there is no corresponding mansion.

This mansion is all about business and financial success.

A good example of how Al Ghafr may work out in a life is the chart of Brazilian supermodel Gisele Bündchen; the Robe can be taken very literally in her case. What strikes the eye in this chart is Mars on the MC, obviously because this has something to do with the profession, with what she will be showing to the world. The aggressive planet is in its detriment so very weak; it means things connected to Mars are not her talent, but the planet will contribute to her career as it is very strong accidentally. This is one of the

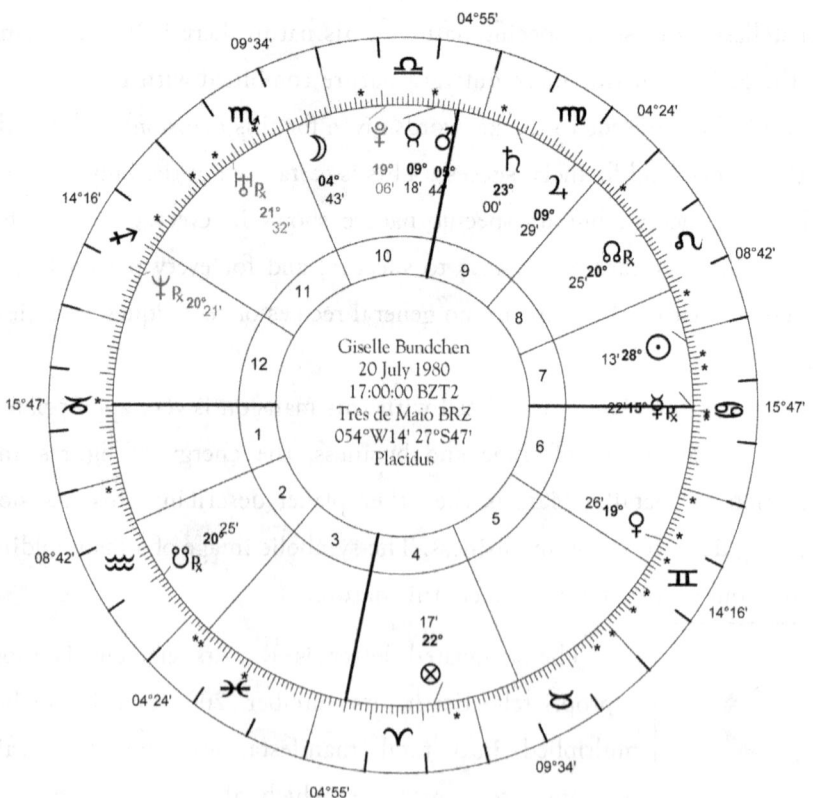

strongest possible placements a planet can have in a chart, so this is not bad for career. It may not be in a good condition but certainly it has lots of power.

Mars is not the planet of outward beauty but it does show up in the career, as apart from the fighting spirit it provides, it indicates the style she initiated. Bündchen's rise to glory marked a change in the world of modelling: it ended the 'heroin chic' style with notorious pale and skinny models. With Gisele Bündchen vitality came back, a healthy look with good curves. Mars will never beat around the bush - it represents the energy of life and action. Her style of cat-walking, and indeed cat-walking is a most important part of modelling, is described as 'stamping', which is also quite martial. This is not just some interesting detail as in fact it played a considerable part in making her the superstar she is.

Mars on the MC is on the star Zaniah on the wing of Virgo, which has a Mercury/Venus nature. This gives Mars more elegance and here Venus is Mars' dispositor; Venus the planet of beauty as Lord 10 shows what she is likely to do as a profession. Venus Lord 10 trines Saturn Lord 1, so this Venus/beauty career is directly connected to her as a person. On the ascendant powerful first-magnitude Wega is placed on the Falling Vulture, the main star of the aesthetic Lyre. It also has a Mercury/Venus nature and is associated with showing divine beauty and harmony in earthly form. The Vulture or the Eagle is falling because it comes down from 'up there' where it has seen many wonderful things which it wants to show to the world.

Like Mars, Mercury is placed on an angle, and planets on angles are always effective in the career. Mercury is Lord 9 of foreign countries, so travelling will play a considerable role in her life. Mercury is connected to Mars on the MC by a mundane square. A mundane aspect is not an aspect by zodiac placement, but by house. Planets in houses, which are not inconjunct or right next to each other, with the same distance to the house cusps are said to be in aspect 'in mundo'. So here Mars on the MC and Mercury on the descendant are at the same distance from the cusp and they are in aspect by mundane square. Note please that the inconjunct is never an aspect as aspects are about the ability of planets to see each other and in this way 'mingle their lights'. Astrology is the science of light, symbolising divine energy. The essential nature of the inconjunct is that inconjunct planets *cannot* see each other and therefore cannot mingle their light (this may have a meaning, but it is not an aspect).

It is interesting to look at the second house of money in her chart as Gisele Bündchen belongs to the group of best-paid super-models in the world. Saturn is the Lord of the second house, it is not the planet of wealth, it has no dignity and it is placed in a falling house which tends to be weaker. This goes to show that money astrologically is a lot more than just the second house; the point is that financial success is always part of a broader success story. If we see a strong chart with a lot of potential for success, more money can be expected; moreover, the second house is not the only financial house. The eleventh house certainly also has to do with the financial position; as the second house from the tenth it indicates what you get paid for your work, your public activities. In Gisele Bündchen's chart Lord 11 is Mars on the MC accidentally very strong.

In her case, however, the lunar mansion certainly also contributes considerably to her success. Not only is Al Ghafr a constellational zone in Virgo with its focus on the Covering or the Robe, literally the central myth in her life, it is also associated with business success. One of the rulers of this part of Virgo is, as mentioned above, appropriately Mercury, the business planet - and this Mercury is in a strong angular position in mundane square with the important Mars on the MC, the other mansion ruler. In addition to this Mercury is conjunct the bright powerful star Canopus, the main star in the Argonaut's Ship, connected to travelling. Canopus is also associated with the Trojan War, which was sparked by a beauty contest among goddesses. This strong placement of Mercury shows she will have a good chance to realise the promises of Al Ghafr.

16. Al Zubana: 16.02 Scorpio – 28.53 Scorpio

Star: Lucida Lancis/The Scorpion's Claw

Arabic letter: Taa

Associated names: The Claws/The Scales/The Business Man

Planets and energies: Saturn/Mars – Wealth/financial success

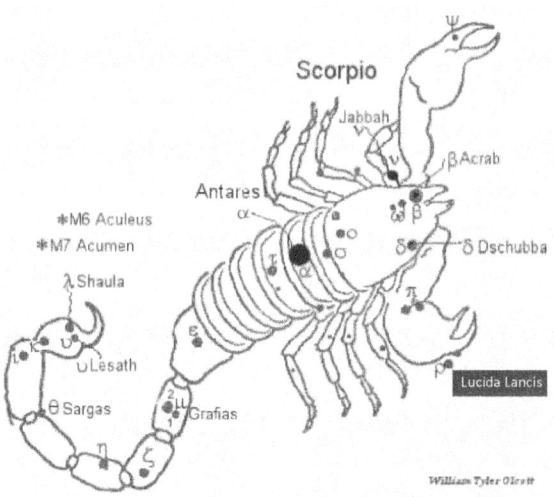

In this sixteenth mansion the Virgo constellational zone is left behind and a very different energy is manifested. Yes, the picture above is correct, this is Scorpio. Al Zubana is Arabic for 'the Claws', of Scorpio of course, but the Claws are also the Scales, so this is Libra too. The truth is that they are the same; the Scorpio Claws *are* the Libra Scales, their instrument, and they are part of the same story of the Scorpion. Libra is said not always to have been a separate constellation. Tradition has it that a long time ago Libra was placed on the pole, but when a new age of the world started, it came down to take up its position as a zodiacal constellation. This is probably connected with the beginning of what the Vedic tradition of India calls the Kali Yuga, the iron era of rampant materialism, spiritual numbness, grave error and suffering. In Christianity this would correspond to the feet of clay and iron of the giant in the famous dream of King Nebukadnezar which was interpreted by the prophet Daniel. This is the period which is currently going through its last most venomous phases, according to some traditional sources; the Kali Yuga has a duration of about 6000 years.

This would mean that Libra 'came down' to the zodiac about 6000 years ago, ending the Yuga of Copper - which is connected to Venus as copper is the metal associated with it. In this Copper Yuga the sign of Venus, Libra, occupied the dominating position on the pole, thus determining the nature of this era. This ended and the Scales from then on were one of the twelve as a part of Scorpio, specifically its Claws. This is a symbolic way of interpreting the Ages the cosmos is going through. The idea of four Ages of an ever-declining quality of life, of an ever-increasing reign of materialism and quantity, is found in all authentic spiritual traditions, not just in Christianity and Hinduism, although in Hinduism it is described more explicitly.

So now the Scales, as the Claws, are part of the story of the killing of Orion, the materialistic brute who was created from an ox-hide and urine. He could be seen as Adam, only made of mud, without the divine breath blown into him. Orion represents the arrogance of matter, and the fact that everything materialistic will eventually die as it is only a shadow of reality and has no substance of its own. Orion, this enormously successful Hunter, bragged he could kill any animal; the gods heard this, were not amused and sent the Scorpion that eventually killed him. On the highest level Scorpio is all about penetrating through the veil of matter in a very decisive and combative way; it is not for nothing that Mars rules this sign in the zodiacal order.

The Scales are the part of the Scorpio zone where justice is done, a verdict is carried out and it is a point of great power. The Claws are the instrument by which this is done. Orion is grabbed and mastery over matter is realised. The opposing mansion is always good to look at too; this is the second mansion, where the creative impulse is entering matter for the first time, but in the sixteenth mansion matter is killed and conquered.

This is the essence of justice, of rebalancing the Scales; anything that does not belong to the eternal order will die. This mansion is the first of four Scorpio mansions, each focusing on a different aspect of the sign.

It is a mansion of power as Orion is killed and mastery over matter is acquired. This is reflected by the planetary energies working here. Saturn and Mars are harsh malefics: Saturn is sacrifice and death, Mars is battle. All the keywords are connected to success and wealth because of the harsh and relentless power of the Claws; it knows how to fight and kill and it will indeed fight and kill. The symbolic image of a ruler seated on a throne holding a scale in his hand reflects this; it bestows the power to deal with the material forces symbolised by Orion. The creative phase is also described  as 'he who Counts', it is said to be connected to the Sky of Mercury, and the letter is Taa, which slightly resembles the glyph for Scorpio. Its number is 9, 3 times the number of the spirit (matter is conquered here), it belongs to the Fire element (the fighting) and it is said to be connected quite appropriately to discernment (for doing justice with the Claws as an instrument).

The corresponding Vedic mansion is associated with an iron will.

This mansion is about the fighting spirit to acquire wealth and success.

A good example of how Al Zubana may work out in a life is the chart of mega-star Beyoncé, who needs no introduction. Success can be seen everywhere in this chart, which is one of the most powerful charts I have ever looked at. Donald Trump's chart is one of the few charts of famous people that seem to be stronger. This illustrates clearly that the chart shows us that our life is a package deal, a life.zip file which is opened when we are born - it is all there from the beginning. The chart is an expression of what we were in God's mind before we were born, but if we are fixated on a bodily form, this is it. We cannot *achieve* success, success is basically given. We cannot *be* Beyoncé; the only level at which we are free is the spiritual and ethical level, but we can always decide what to do and what not to do, so where we focus our minds is very important .

Beyoncé's chart looks very promising, with the immensely strong Venus on the ascendant in its own sign of Libra. Everything she does is connected to this Venus, the singing, the dancing and the fact she calls herself a modern feminist. Venus/Lord 1, the person, is disposed by no one, no one rules her. Libra is one of the signs that, according to tradition, has 'a voice', always an advantage for a singer. Libra is the sign of Air in the swiftly moving mode. Nearby is Pluto which provides this lovely Venus with an overwhelming power, and royal star Spica is close enough to give the Venus power an extra boost. You don't have to be an astrologer to see that this lady is going to do some remarkable Venusian things!

In her solo career she has sold 160 million records, making her one of the best-selling performers ever. Mars is Lord 2 in her radix and is conjunct the expanding Jupiter-like North Node in the tenth house of the profession; it is very strong, proving that in this radix one's wealth can be seen in the second house. Lord 10 of the career is the Moon right on the cusp of the second house, connecting her public activity directly with her financial position. This is good but only moderately so, as the Moon is in its fall and will show up her worst sides - a lack of stability and emotional control which will have a negative effect on her possessions. However, there is so much power in this chart and in this life that this weakness is amply compensated. In addition, the MC is close to royal Pollux, the immortal twin.

There are three planets in the twelfth house of isolation and self-destruction; a lot of planets in this darkest of all houses may give a lot of trouble, but the planets are all disposed by this immensely powerful Venus/Lord 1, which stabilises the potentially more problematic tendencies in her life. A dispositor can improve a weak planet if it is strong itself. The darker side can be felt but she is strong enough to deal with this. An emphasized twelfth house will also to tend make you more sensitive to the astral dimension, and this seems to be true as Beyoncé says an entity called 'Sasha Fierce' takes possession of her before she goes on stage. Is this the source of this strange, smooth glamour? The general significator of women, Venus, and the Sun, general significator of men, are in mutual negative reception as the Sun is in Virgo where Venus has its fall, and Venus is in the sign where the Sun has its fall. By antiscion the Sun opposes Venus over the Asc-Desc relationship axis. Men are creatures that need to be civilised as they tend to harm women, so yes, we can see that she is a feminist.

Al Zubana fits in perfectly. The powerful fighting spirit, the Scorpionic need to kill Orion (men) as the Hunter not only hunts down animals but also women, and there is also this incredible success. Out of the planetary

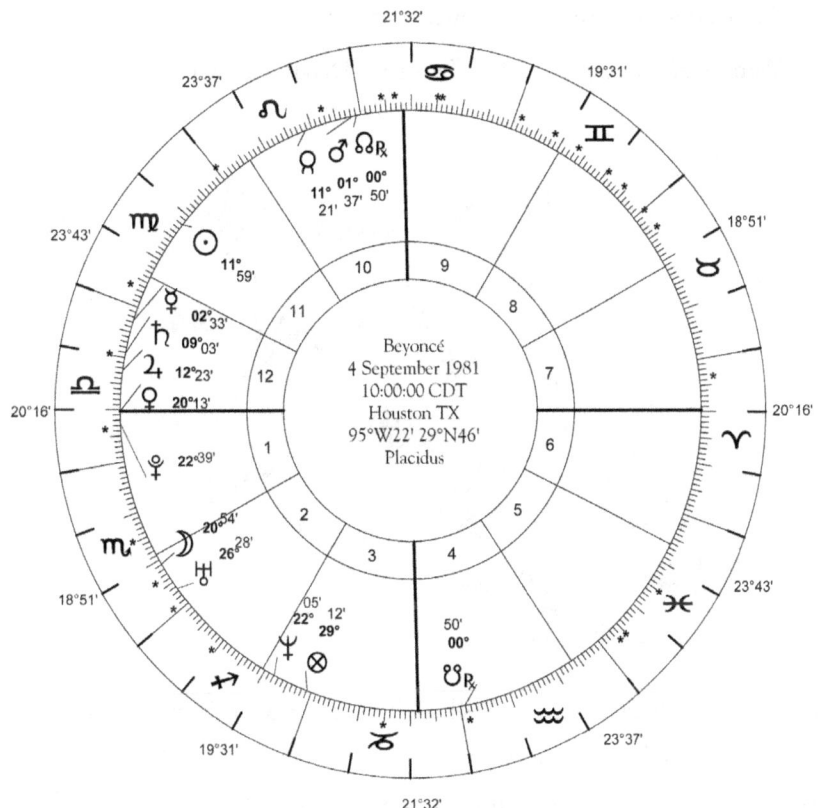

energies working in this mansion Mars is accidentally very strong, so the fighting spirit will certainly manifest. Saturn, the toughness, is essentially strong in its exaltation. This means there is not going to be an unbalanced toughness, so no harshness. The placement in the weakening twelfth house of Saturn means the Mars action side of the mansion will manifest more clearly. To clarify: essential dignity is the measure for the quality of the planet's energy; accidental dignity shows the planet's power to manifest in the world, its 'quantity'.

---

17. **Al Iklil:** 28.53 Scorpio - 11.44 Sagittarius

    Star: Acrab/Dshubba (the Scorpion's Head)

    Arabic letter: Dal

    Associated names: The Crown/The Monkey

    Planets and energies: Mars/Saturn – Driving away enemies/defending

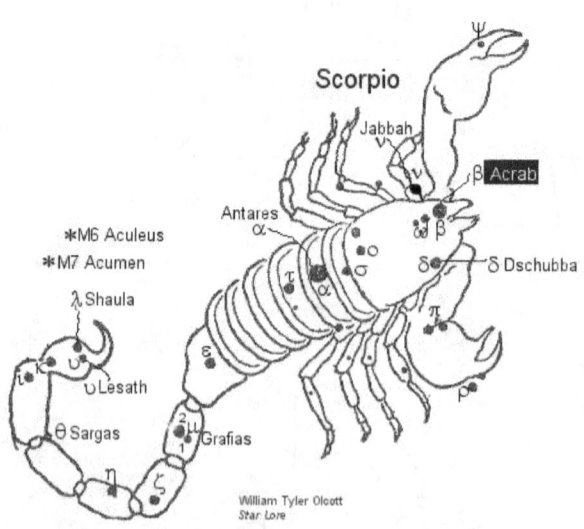

The seventeenth mansion Al Iklil is the second Scorpio mansion and the focus has moved from the Claws/Scales to the head of Scorpio, which gives an indication of its meaning. Claws are connected to merciless action,

The 28 Mansions – Al Iklil

the head more to thinking, so it can be expected that the fierce power of Scorpio will be manifested more intellectually, or at least less in direct action. The same mythological story applies here but in a different form: there is a battle against a gross material opponent and the need to get to the essence behind the veil of appearances, but more in the head. It probably doesn't need saying that Scorpio tends to be radical, expressed not only by the martial rulership of the corresponding sign, but also by its Fixed Water nature, led by fixed emotions.

It can be seen that there is a relationship between the sign and the corresponding constellation; the sign is the origin of the constellation arising from it. They are different astrological factors and they have their places in different cosmological spheres but signs and constellations are family - not brothers but certainly cousins. The general characteristics of the sign will say something about the constellation and its mythological ramifications, but it should be kept in mind that on a practical level a sign is *never* to be associated with a myth. The myth is *only* found in the constellation, and that is why a clear understanding of the precession is essential (see Appendix B).

It is interesting to take a look at the opposite mansion to get an idea of what is going on here in this extended Scorpio zone, 14 mansions back. The third mansion, Al Thurayya, is a Taurus mansion which symbolises the fall into matter, reflecting the fact that here in Al Iklil, at the opposing place, a kind of liberation from material bondage is going on. The name Al Iklil is Arabic for 'the Crown' in other words the head, which needs no explanation. The descriptive stars Graffias (also named Acrab) and Dschubba are found in the head of the killer of Orion, in the animal's brain. The two malefics Mars and Saturn are the planetary energies so we still have a lot of toughness here. A scorpion is not a nice pet.

The keywords all concern protection and guardianship; this is fierce Scorpio attacking and killing the arrogant, brutish Hunter Orion. The symbolic image is a monkey which is not as mysterious as it seems, as the focus is on the head here, and a monkey is always regarded as being very smart. The emphasis has shifted more towards thinking, compared to the preceding mansion of the Claws, which was focused on tough action.

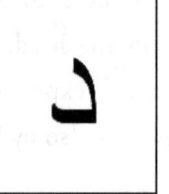

The Arabic letter is Dal with the earthly number 4 and it is said to belong to the Earth element. It is associated with the struggle in our lives to reach the divine essence veiled by matter. This is exactly what Scorpio is doing. The creative step associated with this mansion is 'the Inferior Sky' of the Moon, also called 'the Evident', echoing the tense relationship in this mansion with the material which is the central theme in Scorpio. The next step in the creative process will leave the planetary 'skies' and enter the elemental sphere continuing its downward movement. We have arrived at the border of the material; the Moon is the lowest of the planets, nearest to Earth.

The corresponding Vedic mansion is also associated with protection.

This mansion is all about protection of possessions, defending, preservation and fending off enemies with a focus on mental acuity.

A good example of how this mansion may work out in a life is the chart of the infamous German philosopher Friedrich Nietzsche, who proclaimed the death of God and the birth of the *Übermensch*, the human being who would only rely on himself, and by leaving Christian or any religious ethics behind would grow into some superior being. It is easy to see why the Nazis were attracted to his ideas, although Nietzsche's philosophy is certainly more subtle than its Nazi appropriation. Nevertheless, his ideas were very radical and they represented a fanatical attack on everything that had contributed to European culture up to that point.

The thing striking the eye in this chart is fiery Mars, the ruler of the first house of the person placed in the tenth house of public activity. This is good for fame, the person is 'up there' - it also shows some tough action and battle may be expected. Nietzsche was known as 'the philosopher with the hammer' because he wanted to destroy religion. Mars is on the star Markeb in the Argonaut's Ship, associated with learning and the quest for the Golden Fleece. Lord 10 indicates the profession, activities or themes we play out in public, and Mercury (writing) in a communicative Air sign in mutual reception with Venus can make the writing very attractive. The cusp of the ninth house of philosophy and higher knowledge falls on the cloudy star group Praesepe, the Empty Crib without the divine Child, very appropriate for a thinker fiercely attacking religion in general and especially Christianity. The Sun is the ruler of the ninth house of ideas and it is in the eleventh house, favourable for manifestation in the world.

The Sun is also on royal Spica, a star giving it great success and further increasing its power to manifest. However, the Sun/Lord 9 of philosophy is in fall so the bad side of the Sun will block his connection to God. A bad Sun is pride, showing the human being making himself into a god, exactly the Übermensch, an idea quite in line with the spirit of his times. The Moon is important in the first house of the person and is on another royal star, Antares, the Heart of Scorpio, a powerful purely martial killer star which puts an end to a cycle. This position may raise a question because Al Iklil ends in Nietzsche's birth year (1844) at 9.24 Sagittarius. The Moon is still in the mansion of the Scorpion's Head, but as a planet it is already on Antares, the descriptive star of the next mansion. This situation is discussed below and the solution is that these two functions have to be distinguished from each other as they have different astrological meanings.

The planetary parts as usual have something to add; the Part of Mars, the essence of the martial energy, is conjunct the Übermensch Sun/Lord 9, the hammer philosophy again. Also by antiscion the Parts of Saturn and Mercury are conjunct and a conjunction or opposition of two parts indicates a theme playing an important role in the life. So the Part of Mercury is despair, as Mercury is material detail, the Part of Saturn is imprisonment. How clearly does this describe his godless philosophy, the despairing human being imprisoned in matter? No wonder our Titanic philosopher ended life as a raving madman.

Al Iklil fits in seamlessly. The Scorpion's death blow happens in the head, in ideas, and he is certainly a smart monkey. He seems to be aping God, parading his philosophy as a surrogate religion. Certainly, he is out for the truth behind appearances, but things get turned around. His Orion is not matter but God, a strange reversal, but reversing things is what false prophets do. Mars is essentially the weaker of the planetary energies and this leads to aggression, while Saturn is essentially strong; he knows how to get to the essence of things. Jupiter, the planet of philosophy, is also strong in his own sign, and that is certainly a talent, but he is on the Pegasus star, Scheat, associated with trying to force your way into the Olympic world, trusting your own human strength but with dire consequences.

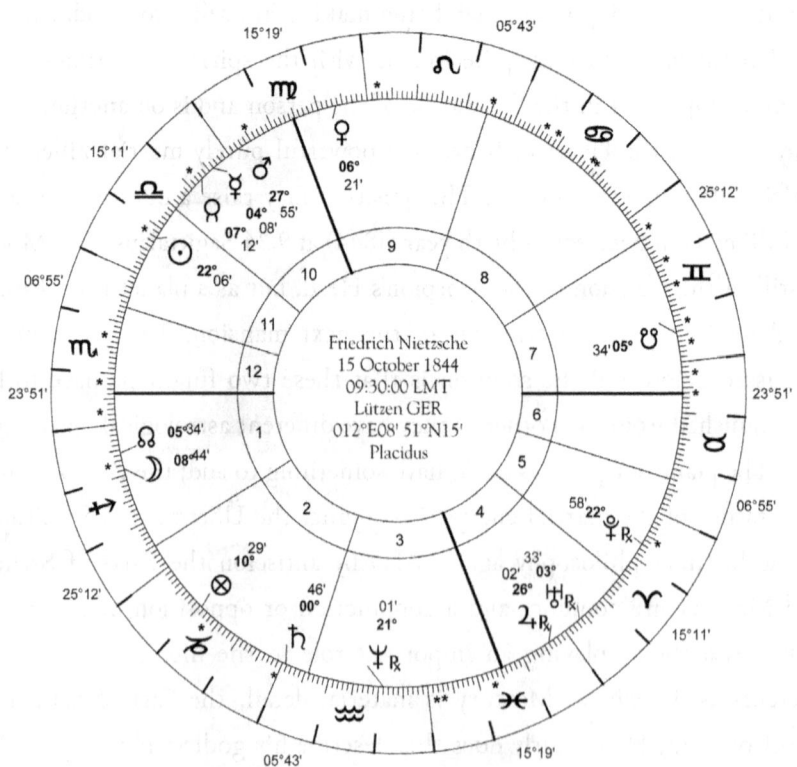

The 28 Mansions – Al Qalb

18. Al Qalb: 11.44 Sagittarius – 24.36 Sagittarius

Star: Antares (the Scorpion's Heart)

Arabic letter: Tâ

Associated names: The Scorpion's Heart/The Snake

Planets and energies: Mars - Defending against enemies/attack/poison/death

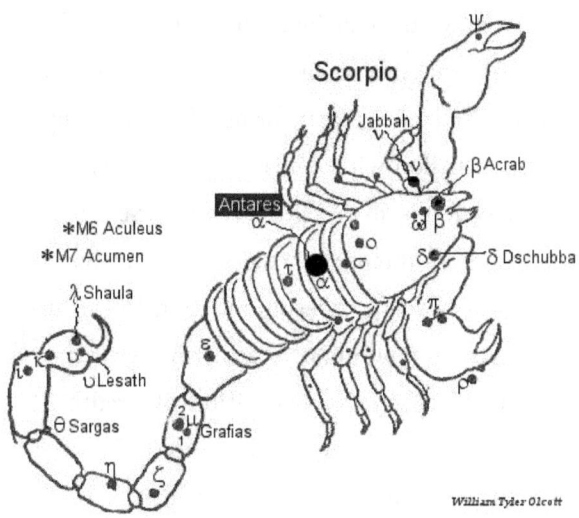

In this eighteenth mansion we reach the essence of Scorpio. The descriptive star is Antares, the Heart of Scorpio, which is what the name of the mansion means in Arabic; the pure intense Scorpio energy is working here. The name Antares comes from 'Anti-Ares', the rival of Ares, and this star is just as martial as Mars himself or perhaps even more so. This is also the third of the four Scorpio mansions: the Claws, the Head, the Heart and the Sting. They are all constellational zones with a clear character of their own. Central star Antares is intensely red, a signature of this most Scorpionic of the Scorpio mansions.

Again there is a slight irregularity which may seem strange at first, as the central star Antares is placed just before the beginning of the mansion. This is not a problem as the star is certainly part of the constellation and is only used to describe the nature of the mansion. As discussed above the division of the circle in 28 zones does not perfectly fit in with the irregularity of the constellations, but perfection cannot be expected at this level of the lunar zodiac. It is a combination of perfect systems (division of 28 parts of exactly equal length) and imperfect groups of visible stars. It does not mean there is anything wrong with the lunar mansions, it only means this is not the solar level of perfection.

As told in the previous mansions, this is the animal that kills Orion, the purely material brute. It wants to eliminate the power of matter, an intention which can take many forms. The opposing mansion is Al Dabaran, a Taurus mansion with Aldabaran as its central star illustrating clearly what this mansion is up to. Aldabaran is the eye of the Bull obsessed by matter, and also of an intense martial red colour, but as the picture of the Bull shows, the fiery energy goes into matter. In this mansion the fiery movement is opposite; conquering or beating matter is the essential theme here. This does not exclude the acquisition of wealth. This is Donald Trump's lunar mansion - the central focus is not on the acquisition of wealth itself but on its protection against opponents and threats.

The keywords are directly derived from this Scorpionic heart: poison, warding off enemies, defending, killing. The associated image is an adder holding its tail above its head, which probably doesn't need explaining; the focus here is very much on danger and killing. The snake is the symbol of the duality of our being, or more psychologically formulated, it's our desire nature. It fits in very well with the sign of Scorpio, which is the element of Water – desire – in a fixed mode. This is the only mansion in the Arabic series associated with a specific medical problem - stomach trouble - because the snake moves on its stomach. The more spiritual process here is that the desire nature symbolised by snake and scorpion should be transcended, the Scorpio should become the Eagle soaring up to heaven, liberated from attachment to earthly things.

The 28 Mansions – Al Qalb

The associated Arabic letter is Taa and its number is 400, the number of earthly frictions multiplied by 100; its element is Air, and here we see the Scorpion killing material attachment to become the eagle. This letter symbolises the state of ecstasy, the discovery and return to God, which is exactly what Scorpio is up to. The creative step is the sky of Ether, the element that is the origin of the other four, and the name is 'He who seizes'. A two-way process can be seen here; the beating of material enemies and acquiring mastery over matter is not only a battle for success but at the same time a return to the higher dimensions. Above Ether the world of the elements is left behind. The parallel Vedic mansion also emphasizes protection and struggle with opposing forces.

This mansion is all about protection, death, defending and eliminating opponents.

A good example of how this mansion may work in a life is the chart of the notorious serial killer Ted Bundy, executed in a US prison in 1989 for his unspeakable crimes. His case immediately raises the question about fate and free will; was he predestined to commit these horrific acts by his chart, or was he a victim of his upbringing and does the chart show this? Can his evil nature be seen? The point of departure of any healthy astrology is that a human being is always free to choose - nobody is ever forced to become a murderer. According to Holy Scripture man is created in God's image and therefore necessarily free. Saint Thomas of Aquine, the "Angelic Doctor" and the most revered teacher of the church in the West, who did NOT condemn the astrology of his time, writes that the human being is certainly *influenced* by the tendencies found in the chart, but he is not determined by them.

So whatever your upbringing, whatever your development, you are always 100% responsible for your choices. You cannot decide that you will be rich and powerful, this is given by the chart, but you *can* decide to be good and then the chart shows the obstacles. Why a human being decides to become a monster like Bundy is a mystery of the soul which cannot be seen in the chart, and this is exactly the free will mentioned above. If you investigate the charts of Nazi war criminals you cannot see they were monsters, but you can read the real circumstances in their lives from the chart very clearly and predict important events in the life.

Although it cannot be seen in a chart if someone is going to be a murderer, some charts definitely look nastier than others. Adolf Hitler's chart is certainly a lot darker than the chart of emeritus Pope Benedict! In Bundy's chart too, evidence of nastiness can be seen accumulating; the first thing we notice is the power of violent Mars disposing three other planets in conjunction with Mercury. This would make Mars the significator of manners as it has a strong influence on the emotions (Moon) and the thoughts (Mercury). Mars is a peregrine malefic without any positive essential dignity, so it will tend to manifest in a more unpleasant way. Mars is also conjunct the South Node, the exit gate of life, on Antares, the Death Star.

Not very nice at all, as this is Mars steering his thoughts and emotions, and it gets even worse, as Mars is in strong mutual reception with Jupiter. Had Great Benefic Jupiter been in good condition with lots of essential dignity, he could have served as a correction for this brooding Mars, but he has none. Jupiter is conjunct the powerful royal South Scale, the merciless Southern Claw of Scorpio, and on top of that, is Lord 8 of Death. So we have the Death Star, the merciless Scorpio's Claw, life's exit gate the South Node, martial aggression and Lord 8 connected to thoughts and feelings. It is getting really creepy now.

Lord 7 of relating to other people only adds to the darkness emerging from this chart. It is Saturn, the Great Malefic, in its detriment showing its nastiest side, retrograde, going against the normal course of things. It is in the twelfth house of isolation, crime and despair on the South Ascellus part of the Praesepe zone, called "the exhalation of piled-up corpses" by the

Chinese. It is also conjunct the Part of the Sun, which is also called the Part of Abundance. This cannot be good with a view to the horrific state of Saturn, as the essence of the Sun is darkened. The twelfth house is the house of demonic possession, a hint of which appears to be quite noticeable in some of his photos.

By antiscion Saturn Lord 7 of relating to others is conjunct Mercury and placed on the first magnitude Centaur star Agena, connected to the story of Pholus who died, because out of curiosity he picked up an arrow which turned out to be poisoned. The arrow didn't look too dangerous but it turned out to be fatal. Mercury in antiscial conjunction with this awful Saturn Lord 7 of others is also conjunct Venus of women, so stay away from this guy! This constellation opposes the Part of Mars, representing

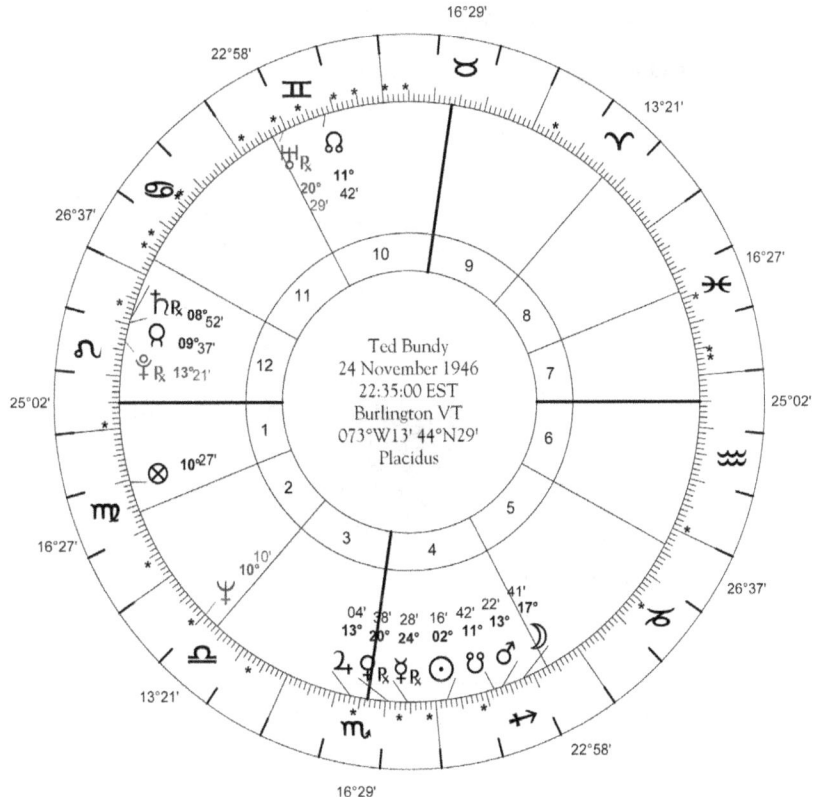

the violent martial essence and indicating some special influence. It's also noticeable that the Parts of Saturn and Mercury are conjunct - this is a particular combination of despair with imprisonment as a special feature.

To all this is added the Al Qalb mansion, itself so strongly connected with killing, and its ruling planets, Jupiter and Mars, indicating how the mansion will manifest, taking us back to the scary significator of manners described above. In January 1989 Bundy was executed by electric chair in Florida State Prison.

---

19. Al Shaulah: 24.36 Sagittarius – 7.28 Capricorn

Star: Shaula/Lesath (the Scorpion's Sting)

Arabic letter: Zai

Associated names: The Angle/The Covered Eyes

Planets and energies: Mercury/Mars – Foresight/protection/siege

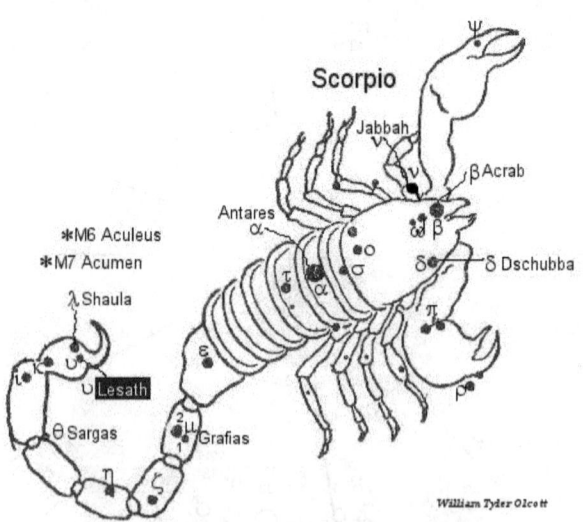

The nineteenth mansion is the last of the four Scorpio mansions; this is the tail of the Scorpio zone and Al Shaulah in Arabic means 'the Sting', requiring no explanation. It is good to realise that tropically Al Shaulah ends in the

The 28 Mansions – Al Shaulah

seventh degree of Capricorn, and the effects of the precession of the whole mansion cycle can be seen clearly here. The mansion falls in the constellation of Scorpio and its star Lesath is even right at the beginning of the mansion, but if we follow the guidelines of many authors and of most texts and apply no precession, this mansion would start much farther back, tropically at about 21° Scorpio. This is near one of the Scales but this mansion is not associated with the Scales, it is the Sting. So how to make sense of that? If we do not precess the mansions, the logic is completely lost.

The mythological story is the same as in the four previous Scorpio mansions, but in mythology there is always a variety of tales. So in one of these varieties brutish Orion is not killed by the Scorpion but by an arrow shot by hunting goddess Artemis, who had fallen in love with him and greatly admired him for his hunting skills. Apollo, Artemis' brother, did not like this and sent the Scorpion to punish Orion, who fled from the dangerous beast by jumping into the sea. Apollo told Artemis that this was the man who had raped one of her nymphs so she shot him, but when she realised what she had done she was broken-hearted.

This is essentially the same myth as previously, only told using different symbols. Apollo is the Sun god and Artemis the Moon goddess. As usual, brother and sister stand for two parts of the soul, and because of her love for Orion Artemis is drawn down to his base, material level. Solar Apollo tricks her into shooting Orion so ending this potentially destructive love connection. The lower part of the soul, the Moon, is saved by the higher part of the soul, the Sun, from falling down into matter by the killing, although Artemis is very sad about this, indicating the soul will always long for this earthy dimension. In this version of the story, we also have a violent killing of an earthbound brute by which the soul reconnects with the pure divine essence behind the material veil.

The stars Lesath and Shaula are found on the Tail of the Scorpion; the mansion's planetary energies are Mars and Mercury - quite appropriate for a sting that injects a lethal poison. The associated keywords are very

Scorpionic: precautions, protection and laying siege. The symbolic image is a woman holding her hands before her face, which reminds us of the Al Terf image, but here it is the approaching Scorpion that is so scary, not the Lion.

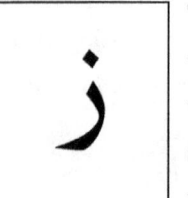 The Arabic letter is Zayin and its number is 7, referring to the seven dynamic cosmic energies also manifesting in the seven classical planets; it is therefore connected with achievement. The letter is also associated with exorcism practised by women (killing the enemy), sincerity (penetrating to the essence behind the material veil) and a process of change; its element is Water. In the creative steps cycle this is the elemental sphere of the Air, and its name is 'the Living' as it is the non-material divine breath from above that gives life. The parallel Vedic mansion is described by the same star and associated with the self-made man who can go through deep crisis and transformation, illustrating the killing theme of Scorpio.

This mansion is all about protection, precaution and laying siege.

A good example of how this mansion may work out in a life is the natal chart of the French populist politician Marine Le Pen. What strikes the eye in this chart is the angular placement of Saturn in the seventh house on fateful star Al Pherg, which is situated in the famous cord that connects the two Fishes. As the two Fishes are a symbol of the two polar forces structuring our world, and in a sense the solar and the lunar energies, the cord is where the world ends. If the Sun and Moon were to be conjunct, the polarity would stop functioning and that would be the end. This is the deepest reason why it is always said traditionally that the Moon cannot overtake the Sun, and the lunar cycles do not fit in perfectly with the solar cycle of a year. As long as they are different the world will continue to exist. In this book we are looking at exactly this; it is the reason we have a lunar zodiac - to manifest the polar tension of the Sun and Moon creating a world.

Al Pherg is a tiny star but it has a lot of influence. In a natal chart it indicates a situation of great importance in the life. In Marine Le Pen's chart Saturn is Lord 4 of the family, specifically the father; it is a malefic in fall so the situation for her at home was difficult. Her father Jean-Marie was an extreme right-wing politician who often triggered violent reactions. Demonstrators used to come to the Le Pen family house and sometimes stones were thrown through the windows. This must have been scary for a young girl. Venus, Lord 1 – Marine in her life – and Saturn are in negative mutual reception. Venus is in the sign where Saturn has its detriment and Saturn is in the sign where Venus has its detriment, so they are extremely harmful to each other.

This difficult Saturn, connected to the family situation in the seventh house, describes very clearly a tendency to close down in relationships with others: in this case, possibly resulting in her being anti-immigration. The Moon indicates as Lord 10 what happens in the public role; it is the general significator of the people and it has just entered its detriment. Such a planet near a sign boundary is always worth some special attention, and this Moon wants to go back into the previous sign where it was much better, so here we can see her resistance to changes in the world that affect French society. She wants to go back to how it was, to make France great again. The Moon is on the star Polis on Sagittarius' bow; there is quite a driving ideological force behind this.

Mars is nasty in its fall, in the tenth house of the public role. Mars squares Saturn so both malefics in very bad condition are connected, combining aggression with harshness; this is not going to be inviting or friendly. The mortal twin Castor is placed on the MC. The Twins are active warriors and Castor is of a mercurial nature, tending to be more flexible or opportunistic. Marine Le Pen reformed her father's unsavoury extreme-right party into a much more socially acceptable movement. Her Sun is very strong in Leo so she knows how to lead. With Venus Lord 1 on the Hydra star Alphard, the essence of the human desire, she is familiar with emotional undercurrents in society, and she can use them politically. The Saturn Part of Imprisonment is conjunct Lord 1, so she connects directly with the very essence of restrictive Saturn.

Al Shaulah with its defensive aggression fits in perfectly; it can be clearly seen how the mansion is the crystallisation point, steering the potential of the chart in a certain direction. Of the planetary rulers Mars is essentially weak in its fall, and that makes the effects of this mansion sharper - as it has a lot of accidental dignity it can still manifest strongly. The other planetary ruler Mercury is peregrine, and side by side with the martial nature of this mansion it introduces a dosage of pragmatism (this reformation of her father's party).

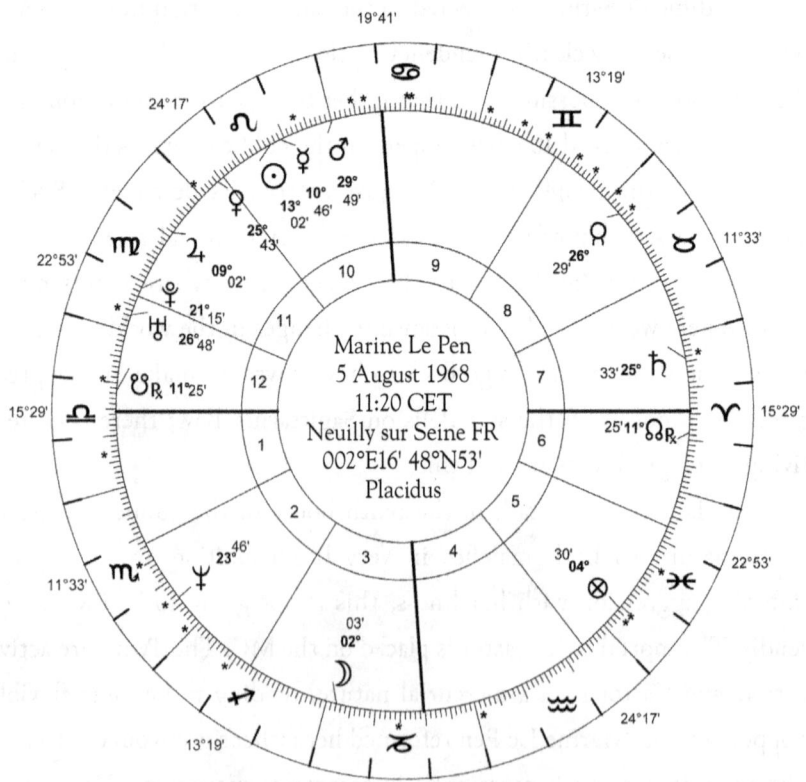

20. Al Na'am: 7.28 Capricorn – 20.19 Capricorn

Star: Nunki (bow, arrow and foreleg of Sagittarius)

Arabic letter: Sin

Associated names: The Beam/The Archer

Planets and energies: Jupiter/Mars – Passionate striving/disciplining and focusing of fiery impulses/activities in nature

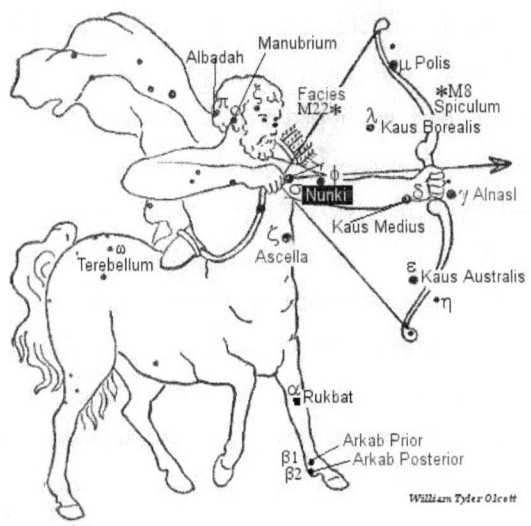

In this twentieth mansion the Scorpio constellation is left behind and the atmosphere totally changes - this is the start of the first mansion of Sagittarius and it is called Al Na'am. This is Arabic for 'the Beam' and it's not too mysterious as it indicates the arrow of Sagittarius, its point of focus. Sagittarius is Chiron, the wise healer and the teacher of many heroes, and certainly knowledge is one of the central issues for him. Chiron with Pholus was one of the few civilized centaurs, an otherwise wild and uncouth race indicated by this mixed nature of man and horse. In most centaurs the uncontrolled horse side has the upper-hand, but Chiron is different, being immortal and thus showing his connection with higher dimensions, although there is always this tension between the human and the animal side.

Symbolically, his parents also express this nature: Chiron is the son of Chronos, a Titan, an earth giant and an opponent of the Olympic gods, and his mother was the Oceanide Phylira. Chronos represents the fall into time and dualistic earthly life, while Oceanides are water nymphs and Water is the element of desire. Phylira however, was seen as one of the civilised Oceanides who taught mankind to make paper and how to write. This basic tension of the horse-man is reflected here in the parents and this is the central point in Chiron's myth; there is knowledge but also the animal nature. Chiron is accidentally wounded by one of the arrows used by Hercules which he had dipped in the Hydra poison, and the Hydra poison represents the essence of the desire nature.

Chiron suffers badly due to the poisoning - he cannot heal himself despite all his knowledge and as he is immortal he cannot die. This symbolically indicates he is overwhelmed by the desire nature of his equine part. To escape the suffering he gives up his immortality and takes the place of the Titan Prometheus, who was chained to a rock in the Caucasus by the gods as a punishment for stealing the fire from heaven and bringing it to mankind. This shows that the stories of Chiron and Prometheus (which means foresight), are very similar. It is all about knowledge and its limitations, the doomed attempt of mankind to become like gods through knowledge. The arrow so strongly emphasised in this mansion is a symbol of the world's axis, the divine centre around which the whole world turns, so again we find the association with higher dimensions.

There is an intriguing connection here with another story full of bows and arrows, the legend of Robin Hood. Everything in this legend is green, symbolising the astral world, the intermediary between the material earth and the divine spiritual worlds, and through this intermediary world arrows – the symbol of the world axis as the divine centre – are constantly fired to connect with God. That is why Robin Hood steals from the rich and gives to the poor - he restores the balance of divine justice in the material world. Robin's meeting with his big companion Little John illustrates this; Little

John is big, like a Titan, representing the Earth power. They run into each other on a bridge (=crossing the desire waters) they fight and Robin has the upper hand. From then onward the Earth power of Little John serves as Robin Hood's ally. Lady Marian (clearly to be associated with Mary, the Holy Mother of God) is the symbol of the soul to be purified in order to give birth to the divine. Both the bow and arrow stories are about making the connection with God, with higher wisdom and knowledge by conquering more material instincts.

The planetary energies in this mansion are Jupiter and Mars; Jupiter is the knowledge trying to connect to the divine in the human part, Mars is the animal driving power. The star describing the mansion's nature is Pelagus or Nunki, placed on the vane of the arrow, so the steering point of the arrow's energies. Its keywords are: high-spirited quest, control of pugnacity, physical endeavour. These clearly reflect the tense connection between the human and the animal sides of Chiron, the instinctive energies which have to be focused on some goal. This rough animal side also shows a connection with nature and outdoor activities. The symbolic image of the Centaur is clear enough. The parallel Vedic mansion has the same themes but adds the maritime dimension, symbolically associated with the control of the desire waters.

Its Arabic letter is Sin. Its number is 60, the three of the spirit doubled in the duality; 3 is the number of returning to the spirit and connected to transcending time. Its element is Water (desire) but sometimes also Fire (purification), and it is said to symbolise the glory of God. It corresponds to 'lowering the wing of tenderness with goodness'. Both descriptions of this letter refer to the connection the arrow is meant to make with God. The letter seems almost graphically to correspond to the image of Sagittarius. The creative step is the Water element.

The Lunar Mansions Guide

In this mansion it is all about controlling instincts and aggression, spreading knowledge, adventuring, outdoor activity, passionate striving and the natural world.

A good example of how Al Na'am may work out in a life is the chart of the still-popular American writer, Ernest Hemingway. Although my recommendation is to judge the chart first and then integrate the mansion's theme, it will be reversed in this case as it is too tempting not to do so. The Mansion of the Beam is a crystal-clear reflection of the important themes in Hemingway's life; it is impressive to see how the natal mansion functions as 'a central control unit'. Hemingway was very much an adventurous outdoor man: hunting, fishing, bullfighting (as an aficionado), sailing - he loved it all. And there was also the other side, which was the communication of ideas. He wrote about all these topics which has made his work timeless – he is still popular in the 21st century.

Every school child probably knows *The Old Man and The Sea* - comfortably short but also an extremely clear expression of the central story of Chiron. The struggle of the fisherman with the natural forces of the sea, the failure to land the fish, the fight with the sharks, it's all there. The fish is the symbol of the divine consciousness but the fisherman fails to bring it ashore, and in the process he loses a large part to the shark - the symbol of desire (like Chiron being wounded by the Hydra's poison arrows). It is striking that the corresponding Vedic mansion literally mentions maritime matters. No doubt unaware of the mythology, Hemingway wrote out the story of his Chiron mansion. Neither Mars or Jupiter have much essential dignity, so the promise of the mansion tends to manifest in a lower, more natural way.

Hemingway was also very much the 'papa', almost a caricature of a masculine man, shown in the chart by Mars placed in the first house of the person. A planet in the first house is seen as the significator of manners describing the behaviour, and this would much correspond with his

The 28 Mansions – Al Na'am

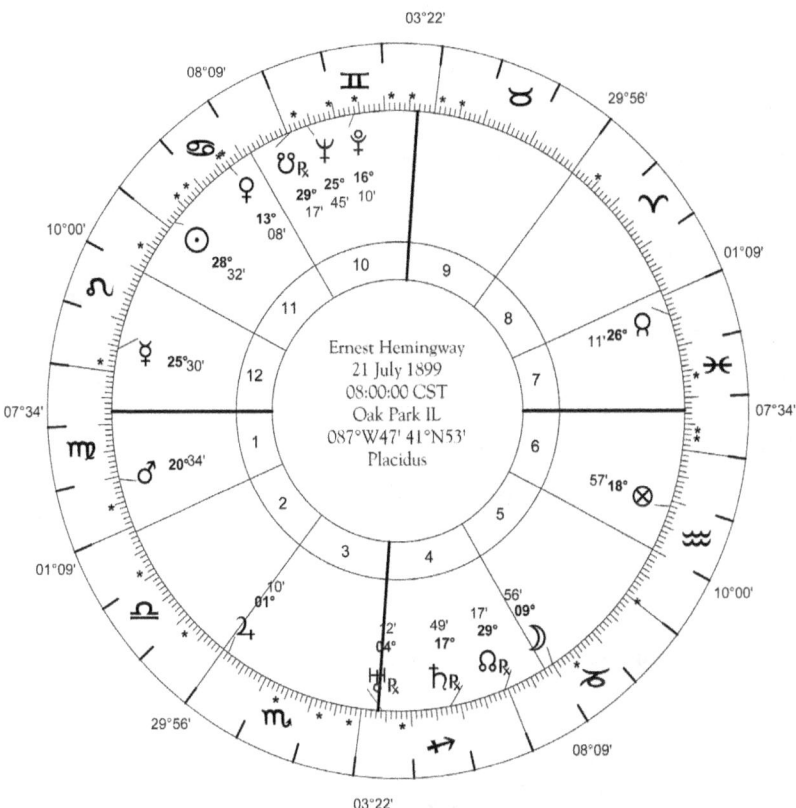

emphasis on masculinity. Mars is in moderately strong mutual reception with Mercury, ruler of the first house of the person and the tenth house of the profession. This makes Mercury, the planet of writing, very important as expression of thoughts is directly linked with the martial fiery energy. Lord 1, 'the person in his life' is on Alphard, the Heart of the Hydra, a direct connection with, or insights into, the undercurrents of the strong human desire nature. Lord 1 is placed in the twelfth house of addiction, so it's not surprising that drinking was also one of his favourite pastimes.

It's interesting that Uranus, the castration by grim Saturn of unlimited potential and freedom you tend to reject, is on the IC, so Hemingway doesn't want to be at home - it's much too boring and he wants to go out. Mars is also Lord 9 of travelling; it is found in the first house, so foreign countries will play an important part in his life. With the arrow of Chiron shot over the horizon, discovering other worlds is clearly part of this, an attempt to find God, lived out on a lower material level. On the MC we find the Hyades. They are the seven half-sisters of the Pleiades who reared Dyonysos, a very promising kid that ended up as an impossible drunkard, literally true in Hemingway's case. Finally, the Hydra poison got the better of him and he gave up his immortality, just like Chiron putting an end to his own life.

---

21. Al Baldah: 20.19 Capricorn – 3.11 Aquarius

Star: Al Baldah (the Hindpart of Sagittarius)

Arabic letter: Sad

Associated names: The City/The Janus Head

Planets and energies: Moon/Mars – Loss/dissension/end

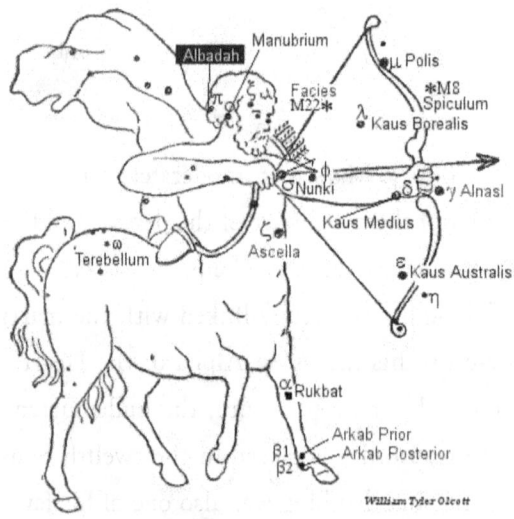

This twenty-first mansion is called Al Baldah, Arabic for 'the City' or 'the District', a name that seems a bit mysterious at first sight. Probably the city could be seen as a symbol for the soul and the district is a part of it, so it would highlight the division and the tearing apart that is the central theme in this mansion. The Arabic astrologer Al Biruni compared this mansion to a desert or a gap, specifically a gap between the eyes of the Centaur, or two eyes that are not connected. That is where the star Al Baldah is found, on the head, near the eyes. Agrippa says it means 'defeat', indicating the same meaning.

The central point here is that the two eyes are not connected; they are looking in different directions, indicating a split. The emphasis on eyes would certainly make sense as the Centaurs were always a tense mixture of human and animal. In the previous mansion this could be focused in the arrow, but in Al Baldah Chiron's two sides seem to be really torn apart. The Hydra's poison that torments him so much and from which he cannot heal himself seems to be getting the upper hand. The two sides cannot be reconciled; it is a house divided against itself. Finally, Chiron gives up his immortality, and this tense situation is left behind. The descriptive star Al Baldah is found in a part of the sky devoid of stars and it is not mentioned in any list of stars relevant to astrology. What we notice, however, is that it is very close to Facies and Manubrium, both nebulous star clusters in the Archer's face and if an archer can't see where he is shooting, it is not very good of course. As Al Baldah is also said to mark the place between the eyes, the conclusion could be that the star is also in the nebulous face and has the same nature as Manubrium and Facies. The nebula in the face causing blindness is another symbolic indication of this tense twofold human-animal nature, the breaking apart of which Al Baldah seems to highlight.

This could easily explain the keywords of discord, tearing apart, hostility, defeat and loss. It also points to the end of one state and the transition to the next. Its symbolic image of a man with two faces reminds us of the Roman god Janus, the god of doors, and the transition from past to future, underlining the idea of division.

The Lunar Mansions Guide

 Its Arabic letter is Sad and it looks a lot like the letter in the previous Centaur mansion. Its element is Water, symbolizing the desire nature strongly present here, and its number is 90, connected to 3, the number of spiritual return at the root of arrow-shooting Sagittarius. Its creative step is "He who kills', pointing at the splitting up into parts necessary in earthly circumstances.

This twenty-first mansion is all about division, tearing apart, conflict, defeat and lack of unity.

A good example of how Al Baldah may work out in a life is the chart of composer Frederic Chopin. First a technical detail: as Chopin was born in 1810 the boundaries of the mansion have to be corrected for the precession, so the Moon is in the first part of Al Baldah (the list in this book gives you the positions in 2000). The first thing we notice in this chart is Chopin's temperament. Always the foundation for the classical psychological delineation, it describes the behaviour in terms of the elements, but also the basic physical build. Elements work on the psychological and the physical level so you can see by their appearance how someone will react; you will know what to expect from a man with a reddish skin and piercing eyes. Astrology is about reality, not just the theory.

The method to assess temperament can be found in my book *Classical Medical Astrology*, so it will not be repeated here. The elements in Chopin's temperament are Earth and Water. He is melancholic-phlegmatic and this combination of elements is very appropriate for a romantic artist; Earth is the concrete form and Water the emotions. It also means he is extremely cold physically as both the elements Earth and Water are cold. This is not good for health as it will make him more susceptible to cold diseases. On the sixth house cusp Mercury is placed in sextile and negative reception with Saturn Lord 6 of illness, so the illness theme is very much indicated here. Mercury is one of the significators of the lungs and Chopin died of a lung disease, probably tuberculosis, a very cold disease. It would have been good for him to take heating foods and herbs as a preventive measure to balance him more.

His susceptibility is further enhanced by the fact that Mercury Lord 1 of the body is on cusp 6, right on the high-energy line of the illness house - but the malefic South Node on the ascendant by antiscion, and Pluto and the Sun opposing the ascendant (the body) do not help much either. These positions also indicate his stormy relationship with George Sand, a feminist; she was a very masculine woman. Pluto and the Sun near the descendant describe this dominating partner so there was quite a polarity between her and this sensitive phlegmatic-melancholic romantic

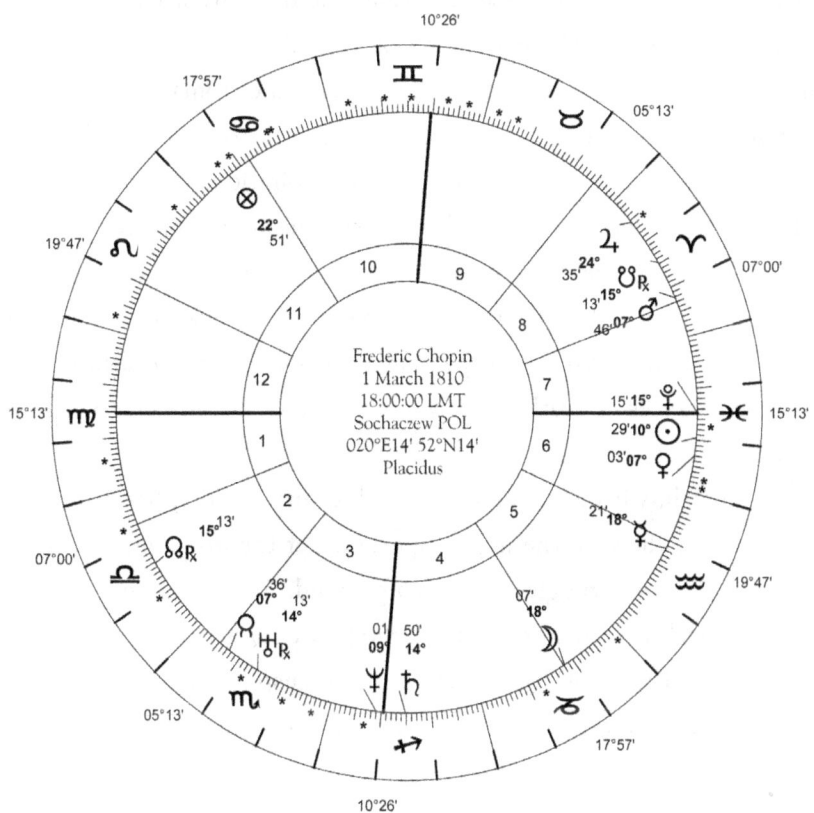

musician. Venus, the planet of love, strong in its exaltation is nearby and probably prevented them from splitting up right away.

The eye is also drawn to the IC, the family. Chopin was born in Poland but he lived in exile in France because of the unstable political situation in Poland. Neptune (chaos) is right on the IC, malefic Saturn is in the fourth house and Lord 4 of the home is Jupiter in the eighth house of death, and on the star of fate Al Pherg. Al Pherg is part of the Pisces constellation symbolising the end of the cycle. His Polish descent was an important theme in his life; he used many Polish folk musical motifs in his compositions. As George Sand said, he was also an enthusiastic patriot, the lost homeland being one of the dominating themes in his life.

His musical talent is indicated by the exalted Venus; exaltation tends to exaggerate, so this describes the romantic quite well. On the cusp of the fifth house of creativity is the Moon; the planet of the emotions is in a deplorable state of detriment, providing some nice romantic material for Chopin to work with. By antiscion this Moon is conjunct the IC, again indicating the lost homeland as a source of inspiration. Venus is also Lord 9 of religion. Chopin was a Catholic by birth but did not practise his faith; Venus is combust and in the sixth house, so not very strongly manifested. However, he died peacefully, returning to the faith of his youth in his final hours. This is indicated by a very strong Mars on cusp 8 of death, showing the circumstances of death. This Mars is Lord 3 of really practising your religion.

Al Baldah, with its connotations of loss and conflict, fits in very well with this life, showing the huge importance of the lost Polish homeland and the fiery love struggles with George Sand. The Moon and Mars are associated with this mansion, quite appropriate for the fierce emotions of a romantic artist, the Moon in detriment on cusp 5 of creativity showing there is some material to work on. A tormented soul is an artist's goldmine.

Last Quarter of Seven Mansions

22. Al Sa'd al Dhabhi: 3.11 Aquarius – 16.03 Aquarius

Star: Dabih (Capricorn's Eye)

Arabic letter: Za

Associated names: The Lucky One of the Slaughterers

Planets and energies: Saturn/Venus – Sacrifice/liberation/spiritual advance

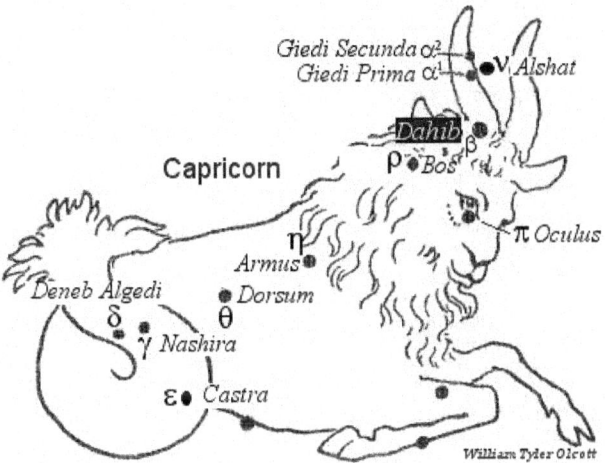

This mansion is the start of the fourth and last quarter of the mansion cycle, and in the order of the zodiac Capricorn is associated with winter and death. Al Sa'd Al Dhabhi in Arabic means 'the Fortune of the Sacrificer', so it will be clear this it is not really a fun mansion. The Goat-Fish which is the central theme here is generally not well-understood, but the fact that it is often found on antique grave monuments points the way to its meaning. It has to do with death and with the transformation to another state, in the broadest sense of the word. According to the old texts Dabih is the eye of the Goat-Fish indicating a strong focus on the next life; the Goat-Fish is looking at the phase that is to come after death.

The mythological story of Capricorn emphasizes the same theme. This story is about Pan, god of the wild, who is walking with his flute through the woods, enjoying the natural beauty and hoping for a nice nymph to appear, but instead he runs unexpectedly into Typhon. Typhon is a horrible monster with a body consisting of snakes. As snakes are symbols of duality, Typhon can be seen as Death. When human beings enter earthly life, they enter duality and this means at some point they will die; everything will finally return to the divine unity, as nothing can exist on its own in a stable form. In Christian theology this is described as the original sin; Adam and Eve became separated from God as a result of their actions, and from this situation was created illness and death.

Typhon represents Death and naturally Pan tries to get away - he jumps into the river and changes into a fish, making the Goat-Fish a symbol of transition. The Goat-Pan part is the natural life, forced by the confrontation with death to make a transformation to the next phase, which is the Fish. The Fish is a symbol of higher things, as illustrated by Christ as Ichtos; the Fish is a well-known symbol of a more spiritual state. A fish is detached from desire, symbolised by the fact that it thrives in the Water element (the element of desire) that will take the life of other creatures. It is also said that a fish never sleeps; its eyes are always open, pointing to the higher consciousness that transcends earthly duality.

The word 'panic' is derived from Pan because he used to scare everybody by making strange noises in the woods, indicating the dark side of the sensual life in the body for which he stands. It may seem attractive but there is something scary about it because you can't see what is hiding in the woods producing these noises. The confrontation with Typhon makes clear that the earthly body is not a safe place and the only way to survive is to change into another state, as Pan himself so clearly illustrates. That the panic breaks out at midday is symbolic too, as the Sun is at its highest point and things can only go down from there – you start to see the point of sunset. The message is to let go of earthly attachments before they are

The 28 Mansions – Al Sa'd al Dhabhi

taken away from you. This is the reason this mansion is associated with 'the Sacrificer' or 'the Slaughterer'. Pan's change into a fish to save his soul cannot be realised unless a sacrifice is made.

The descriptive star is Dabih, the Fish-Goat's Eye fixated on the afterlife, although there is also a star in Capricorn called Oculus, which is Latin for eye and marks the other, right eye. It is interesting that in medieval churches an oculus can be found too - it is a hole pierced through the thick church wall, through which you can see the light outside. This exactly indicates what the main theme is here, seeing the light above through the wall of matter by making a sacrifice (in church). The planetary energies are said to be Mars and Venus, but Dabih itself is described as a Saturn-Venus star which seems to be more appropriate as the sacrifice of Pan and sensual attachment are the central themes here.

Its keywords are perfectly understandable from this story: sacrifice, leaving prisons, severing earthly bondage, transformation under high pressure – it is all about escape from material restriction. Its image is a man with wings on his feet and a helmet on his head. The wings of course refer to an escape from earthly limitations and the helmet reminds us of Perseus, who wore one to make him invisible so that he could kill Medusa, the essence of the desire nature. The symbolism is quite clear – the earthly form is left behind. This is the lunar mansion in the charts of Pope Francis (the sacrifice) and German Chancellor Angela Merkel (the escape in her case is the *Wende*; she grew up in the communist East but rose to power in united Germany, the defining story in her life).

The associated Arabic letter is Za in which the focus on the next phase can be seen almost graphically again; this shows that in Arabic, as in Hebrew, letters are the building-blocks of creation. Its number is 900 - 3 x 3 x 10. 3 is the number of the return to God and is said to symbolise the manifestation of the divine. It corresponds to 'the suppression of the Satanic state', which is of course in line with the Capricorn story described above. The creative step is the Minerals, pointing to the earthly form that can be left behind here.

There is no parallel Vedic mansion, at least not one connected to the Capricorn myth. The twenty-second Vedic mansion is associated with an extra-zodiacal constellation which happens more often in the Vedic series than in the Arabian cycle. In the Vedic cycle this is the Eagle of which Altair is the main star; the majestic king of the birds soaring up to heaven to see how it is up there. It is essentially the same theme, and although the whole sacrificial dimension is not emphasized in the Eagle myth, this can be explained by the cultural differences between these two civilizations. As Europe is the part of the world where material petrification is at its worst, far-reaching measures are called for to liberate the human being from his material bondage. It should be realised that the boundaries of the Arabic and Vedic mansion are not the same; the systems are similar but not identical (see Appendix A).

In this mansion it is all about liberation, escape from prison, sacrifice, the after-life, confrontation with death.

It will be clear that there is a strong religious connotation in this mansion as 'the Sacrificer' is Pan giving up his sensuality to escape death, which is the ultimate illustration of man's weakness and dependency on God. However, this certainly does not necessarily work out in a spiritually positive way, as this is also 'the Fortune of the Slaughterer'. It may well manifest in a confused and distorted way as can be seen in the chart of the notorious cult leader and murderer Charles Manson. His story is well-known. He and his group were involved in several murders, most notorious of which is the murder of actress Sharon Tate, the then pregnant wife of film director Roman Polansky. Manson was convicted for his crimes and died in prison in 2017.

The 28 Mansions – Al Sa'd al Dhabhi

The first thing we notice in his chart is that Jupiter, the planet of religion, is on an angle and is also Lord 9 of spirituality and Lord 12 of isolation crime, magic and imprisonment - and yes Manson did spend a lot of time behind bars. He was also a cult leader with a connection to Scientology, the sinister brainchild of Lafayette Ron Hubbard. Most people don't know that Hubbard was not only an SF author and the inventor of Scientology, he was also deeply involved in the most hideous black magic, working closely with people like Aleister Crowley and rocket scientist Jack Parsons. That Charles Manson would have been interested in the occult can also be seen in this angular Jupiter, and in his role as Lord 12 of magical techniques.

With two planets on the descendant, Manson would be able to manifest himself powerfully and there are even two other planets the Sun

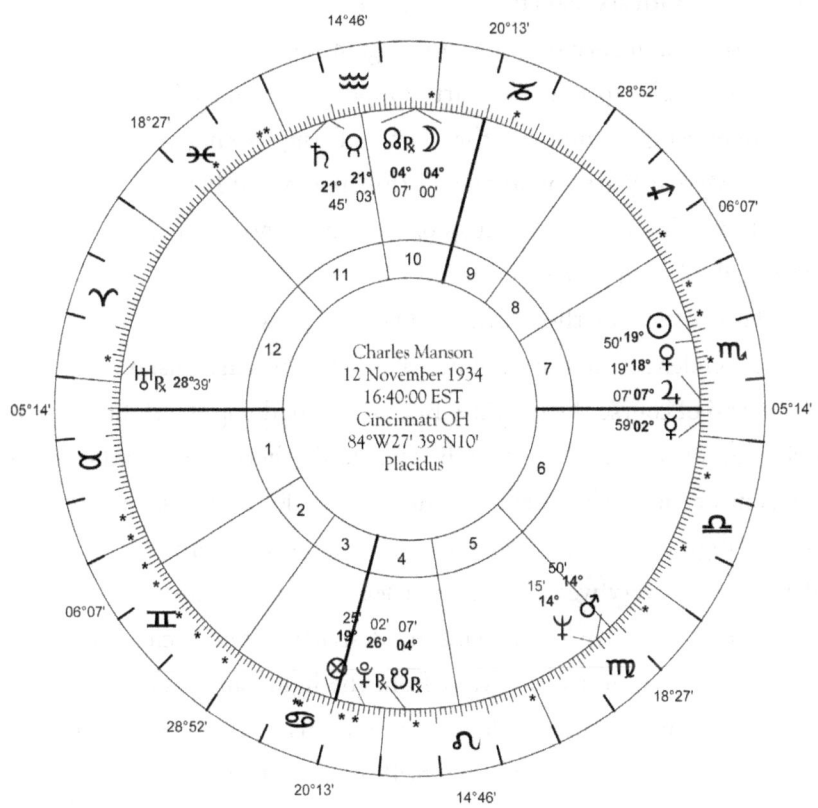

and Venus/Lord 1 in the seventh house, so he will interact very strongly with others. Venus Lord 1, (Manson 'in his life') is weak in its detriment showing its worst sides and it is also combust. He will be harmed by everything the Sun stands for; in this context the Sun can be, among other things, the authorities. Venus/Lord 1 is on Unukalhai, the poisonous Heart of the Snake (the Snake essence) and the Sun is on the North Scale, one of the Scorpion's Claws, the executors of Justice.

Also striking is the position of the Moon, general significator of families and Lord 4 of families on the expansive North Node, very strong in the tenth house. His cult was called the Manson 'Family'; the Part of Fortune, the hunger, is on the IC, so yes - this is what he wants so much. In the eleventh house and also very good for manifestation in the world, Saturn/Lord 10 is found in very good condition and conjunct the Part of Abundance. With six planets in strong places it is clear this person is going to exert some influence on the world. Again the planetary parts, as strong motives, have a lot to add. The Part of Jupiter is on the MC, strengthening the Jupiter/religion motive, the Parts of Imprisonment (Saturn) and Despair (Mercury) are conjunct, and this manifested literally. The Part of Venus/Love/Union is on the cusp of the eighth house of Death conjunct Antares, the Death Star - that is quite scary.

The mansion of the Sacrificer fits in very well; there is the strong religious tendency, the theme of death and difficult circumstances pushing you on, and of course the sacrifice. But instead of doing the right thing and sacrificing his own desire nature, he sacrificed others like a heathen priest. Mars, one of the planetary energies in this mansion, is not strong, it has no essential dignity so it tends to work out in a more malefic way. The other ruler, Venus, is very weak and cannot let go of Pan's sensual attachment. It did not end well. A lot of Manson's destructive tendencies can be seen here but the decision to turn away from the light cannot be seen and the decision to commit these hideous crimes, this is the free will: you can always say no to whatever presents itself in your life.

23. Al Sa'd Bula: 16.03 Aquarius - 28.53 Aquarius

Star: Al Bali (the Left Hand of Aquarius)

Arabic letter: Tha

Associated names: The Good Fortune of the Swallower/The Dog-Cat/The Hybrid

Planets and energies: Mercury/Saturn – Devouring/destruction/loss

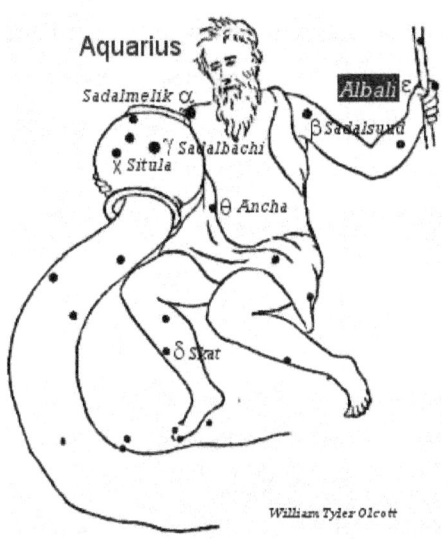

This is the first of three Aquarius mansions and its name in Arabic means 'the Fortune of the Swallower', which is a bit mysterious (see further below). The constellation Aquarius is, in one version of the story, associated with Ganymede, the most beautiful of mortals, who was carried to heaven by the Eagle to serve as cupbearer to Zeus. The beauty mentioned here should of course be understood as a symbol, indicating the closeness of Ganymede to the divine world. The same thing is indicated by the famous jug in which Aquarius keeps sweet water; it is the only one of twelve zodiacal constellations in which sweet water is found, and sweet water is symbolically controlled desire. Salt water indicates wild, undisciplined desire. This sweet water, the disciplining of the human desire nature, is a preparation for the next phase, spiritual rebirth.

This next phase is symbolised by the pouring out of the water by Aquarius. Eventually it streams into the mouth of the Southern Fish - a fish being a symbol of realised higher consciousness, as was explained in the myth of the Sea-Goat. In both versions of the story there is a purification process going on, ending up in the pacifying of the unruly soul and spiritual realisation, but *eventually* is probably the key to understanding this first of the three Aquarian mansions. The process begins here and it is a precarious business; the water is not yet refined and sweet as this will be realised only in the next two mansions, but this is the early phase in Al Sad Al Bula. It may lead to problems indicated by the particular place of its descriptive star Albali, on the left hand of the Water-Bearer. The left, in Latin *sinister,* always has a negative meaning; it is the dark, wrong side. Going from the dark left to the bright right side would certainly reflect the process of taming the Waters as they pass through these three mansions; this process has to be carried out in the soul, with nobody watching, which is why Aquarius stars are also associated with secrets.

The descriptive star Albali can be seen as the start of the process when the water is still salty and wild; the planetary energies working in this mansion are Mercury and Saturn. Its keywords are very negative; they include hunger, shrinkage, contraction, separation and deprivation, to be understood by this position on the left-hand side. The start of the distillation of the wild water of the desire nature is dangerous - the process does not yet have a firm basis, and it is easily disrupted and corrupted. The force of the salt sea water may overwhelm the person so that things will not be held together. Controlled by the desire nature, the distiller will become the swallower, explaining the name.

The symbolic image is clear; it is a dog's head on a cat's body, an unstable combination of opposites. The associated letter Tha is said to represent consolidation, exactly the thing this mansion is trying to achieve. Its number is

The 28 Mansions – Al Sa'd Bula

500, the 5 indicating the human control over the other four elements. Its element is Water, indeed the focus point in this Water-bearing mansion. The creative step is associated with the vegetable kingdom, and is called 'He who nourishes'. Aquarius in the end will pour out the waters for the people. There is no parallel Aquarian mansion in the Vedic system.

In this mansion it is all about devouring, loss, divorce and a strong tension between two foreign elements.

A good example of how the mansion of 'the Good Fortune of the Swallower' may work out in a life is the chart of Maxima Zorreguieta, who married the Dutch crown prince Willem-Alexander and who is now the Queen of The Netherlands. Queen Maxima was born in Argentina and she brought some South-American flamboyance and charm to the Dutch royal family, which has made her very popular. She comes from a good family; her father served in several Argentinian cabinets as Secretary for Agriculture. This caused big problems in The Netherlands as it happened during the cruel junta years and her father was held responsible for these cruelties, although he seems not to have been directly involved. As a result he was not allowed to be officially present at his daughter's wedding with the crown prince.

These problems and secrets in her family can be seen clearly. Jupiter, the planet of the elite, is Lord 4 of the family you grow up in and it is strong in its own sign - a good family. However, Jupiter is placed in the twelfth house of secrets and is conjunct Neptune, a factor that tends to spread chaos; Poseidon is not a very nice guy at all. Before looking further at the other planets, it's a good idea to delineate the planetary parts to show how important they are in a life. You cannot do without them! For example, by antiscion the Part of the Moon, the very essence of the lunar energy is conjunct the Part of the Sun, the very essence of the solar energy, yes king and queen!

If there is a conjunction or opposition of two parts, the themes that can be associated with the parts will play an important role in the life, but to do this they do not need to be connected to another radix factor. This importance of relationships is reflected yet again on the descendant by a conjunction of the Part of Mercury with the Part of Venus, also by antiscion. The Part of Mercury symbolises a very difficult choice that has to be made and the Part of Venus is the Part of Love. So this conjunction of these Parts on the descendant of relationships points to an important choice to be made in love; marrying a crown prince is not an easy decision.

There is even a third conjunction of the planetary parts by antiscion, of the Parts of Saturn and Mars. This symbolises imprisonment (Saturn) and the courage (Mars) to deal with it; it points to the golden cage this marriage also is, and that she has the courage to live in it. As the parts move very fast their positions are very, very individual and they are very specific for this person. Somebody born two minutes later would not have them in their chart. Having many activated planetary parts as in this chart can often point to a special life.

Lord 1 in this chart is Saturn and its position is certainly striking, tightly conjunct the Sun, so combust; she is totally overwhelmed by the royal Sun, as yes, she is married to a king! This conjunction is on Algol, often called the most malefic star in the heavens, so how could we interpret that? Algol is not only pure disaster, it is also strongly connected to glamour. Algol is Medusa, an ugly monster with snakes as hair, but Medusa is also often depicted in another form, a very seductive woman. These are two sides of the same coin. The snakes on the head are symbols of desire controlling the thinking, so this points to losing your head as clear thinking stops, but you can also make others lose their heads; this is the royal Algol glamour that Maxima certainly enjoys. The Sun/Lord 1 conjunction squares the Moon/Lord 7 of relationship, emphasizing the royal marriage theme.

Venus in its detriment in Aries is in sextile with the general signficator of the emotions, the Moon, and disposes (has power over) the general significator of thinking, Mercury. This means Venus is the significator of

The 28 Mansions – Al Sa'd Bula

manners, as it strongly influences thoughts and feelings. Venus is charm of course, and its detriment does not take away the nature of the planet, but it does change its focus. It is not really the emotional, loving connection Venus can give here, it is more the lovely appearance. In Queen Maxima's case this is shown, apart from her unmistakable charm, by the *haute couture* she tends to wear, often drawing a lot of attention. The significator of manners describes very much how you present yourself.

But how on earth does this mansion of 'the Good Fortune of the Swallower' with its strong negative connotations of waste, divorce and loss, fit in with the life of this glamorous girl from Argentina who married the Dutch crown prince and became the Queen of the Netherlands? This case is included exactly to show that things are not always obvious; sometimes we have to look again and it is never a good idea to rely on keywords too

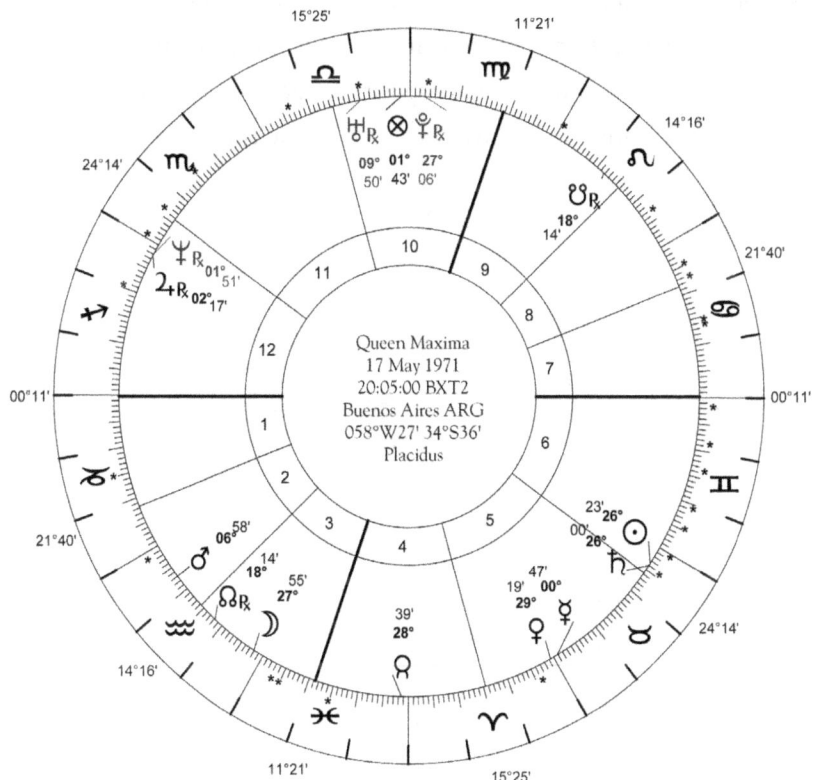

much. The mansion image of the 'dog-cat' shows a union of two quite foreign parts; she had to give up her own life and her freedom to come to live in the cool, windy and wet Netherlands. She had to fit into the Dutch royal family and relate to the Dutch people, all elements totally strange to her. So yes, the union of cat and dog is there, and this is the most important situation in her life. There is also the aspect of the Swallower here, as she seems to indulge in the glamorous jet-set luxury side of a royal life (and not every royal person will).

Can it be seen how this will work out? Will the mansion show its worst sides or is it going to manifest in a milder way? The planetary energies in this part of Aquarius are Mercury and Saturn and if they are in bad condition the mansion can be expected to show its less agreeable sides. Mercury has a little essential dignity by face, weak but much better than nothing at all. Saturn has medium dignity by face and term, not strong but much better than nothing. So the energies in the mansion can be manifested in a milder more positive way. Had the planets been in detriment or fall this would have been more difficult.

24. Al Sa'd al Suud: 28.53 Aquarius – 11.45 Pisces

Star: Sadalsuud (Aquarius' Shoulder)

Arabic letter: Dhal

Associated names: Luckiest of the Lucky/Foster Mother

Planets and energies: Saturn/Mercury – Fertility/growth/opportunities

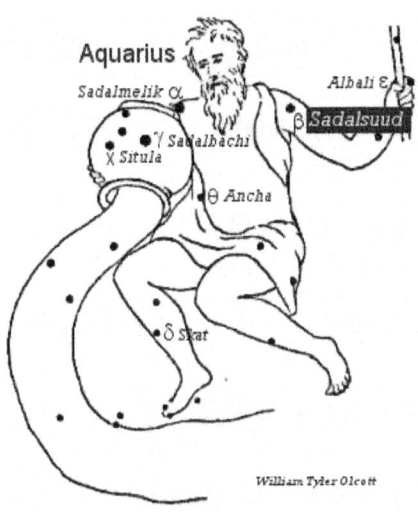

The next phase of Aquarius starts in the twenty-fourth mansion. This is the Water-bearer's shoulder and compared to the left hand it indicates a more stable condition. This is reflected in the name of the mansion which in Arabic is 'the Luckiest of the Lucky'; the negative connotations of the previous mansion are gone. Here the process of the distilling of the raw salt water is in full force and the fruits are ripening - the sweet water can be poured out now to everybody's benefit. Most appropriately the star with the same name was always associated with a period of gentle, fertilising rain. The shoulder is also the place where the jug is carried, so it all seems to be in place here now.

The water in Aquarius is a stream that ends in the Mouth of the Southern Fish, signifying spiritual rebirthing, and the star Fum-al Hut is the Fish's Mouth, the star of Christmas, so Aquarius is a kind of preparation phase, as previously explained. Something is going to be given out to others which is meant to benefit them in their development, and this is connected to the spiritual destination indicated in the Southern Fish. As it is about sweet water, it may be expected that this is associated with higher learning; this is meant to enable people to control their baser natures, but doesn't always mean it will be done successfully. Every mansion can have less pleasant effects; the dignities of the planets will give some indication about this.

The planetary energies working in this mansion are Saturn (discipline) and Mercury (detail) and they describe the purification process of the Water quite well. The image in this mansion does not leave too much to be explained - it is a woman breast-feeding her child, so the whole idea of feeding and nourishing is much underlined here. It clearly corresponds with this stream of pure sweet Water prepared by the Water-bearer; its activities should always be seen in the perspective of the Water streaming into the mouth of the Southern Fish. It is interesting to note that the 24th mansion in the Vedic series is the only Aquarius mansion in that cycle, and its central theme is the process of humanisation, of controlling and purifying the desire Water too. In the Vedic tradition this Aquarius mansion is associated with higher knowledge in the form of astrology/astronomy but also very literally with aviation (Aquarius is also Ganymede, who is taken up to Olympus by the eagle). This intertwining of the literal and the symbolic is quite typical for stars and constellations.

Aquarius is known as the most human sign, which can be understood from this process of distilling the Water. Before any real connection with the spiritual dimension can be made, the human being has to become really human, so leave behind his animal side as much as possible. If someone is totally controlled by the desire nature, the door to the spirit cannot be found and opened. This also explains why Saturn, the planet of discipline and sacrifice, is the ruler of the sign of Aquarius. Constellations and signs

The 28 Mansions – Al Sa'd al Suud

are different and should be clearly distinguished from one another, but they are also related - not identical but similar. It will not come as a surprise then that the keywords in this mansion are very positive: accumulation, spreading, expansion, advantage, support. The creative step is 'the animals', as their nature is controlled here.

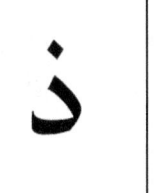

The Arabic letter associated with this mansion is Dhal, and its number is 700, which represents all the seven dynamic forces (the planets), and their fullness in the cosmos (multiplication by 100). It is said to belong to the Fire element, referring to purification (Fire burns away the desire water). It symbolises the heart of ideas and the knowledge of languages, reflecting the connection with knowledge by distilling the essence.

In this mansion it is all about growth, fertility, feeding and increase.

A good example of how this mansion may work out, are Joe Biden's progressions at the time he was elected as the US president. The secondary progression of the Moon passing through the lunar mansions indicates the developments someone is going through, but as always, this should be judged in the context of the situation. In analysing the progressions in the traditional way, the movements of the Luminaries (the Sun and the Moon), the angles (primary directions of the ascendant and MC) and the Parts of the Luminaries (the Part of Fortune and the Part of the Sun) will be investigated. These are the most important factors and you do not need much more to see the main line of development in a life. The first thing we notice in Biden's progressions in November 2020 is the MC moving over Antares, the intensely red and martial Heart of Scorpio, "burning bright in the forests of the night" (William Blake). Antares as the Heart of the Scorpion is its essence, an extremely powerful killer-star. The Scorpion is the poisonous beast sent by the gods to finish off the very successful but boastful, arrogant Hunter Orion; it is the Death Star, ending cycles.

Here the subtlety of the delineation of the stars can be seen, because the question is who or what is going to be put to an end? Will it be Biden's own career or will *he* be the Scorpion dealing the death-blow to an Orion? It is all about roles. To see Donald Trump as Orion in this story seems obvious, so this means Joe Biden will kill Orion-Trump. In working with the fixed stars the associated myth is always of crucial importance. Your role in the mythological scenario, given by the context, determines how the prediction will turn out; if you know your stars, you can even consciously try to emphasize the more positive role in the story.

Other progressed/directed positions on bright important stars confirm Biden's victory. The Part of Fortune is near Achernar, the powerful benefic and successful Mouth of the River, a star of a Jupiter nature with undertones

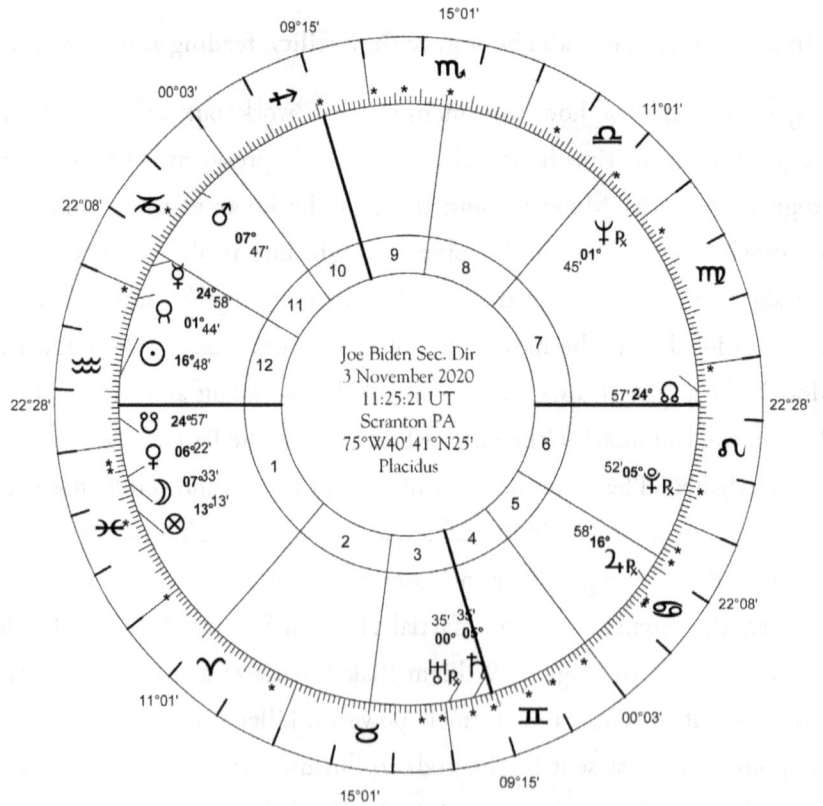

of usurpation; Orion-Trump accused his killer-Scorpion of having stolen the elections. A myth can show itself in many ways. The Part of the Sun (the reversed Taurus symbol) is on Altair, the main star in the Eagle, the royal bird soaring up to heaven. The Part of the Sun represents the solar essence, quite relevant to an aspiring president. Because of its formula (Asc + Sun – Moon) it moves backward through the signs. So it will soon enter Capricorn, activating its ruler Saturn. Saturn is strong in Biden's natal chart placed on Aldebaran, the mighty red Bull's Eye.

The movement of the secondary progressed Moon through the lunar mansions completes the positive picture. At the moment of his victory the Moon was in Al Sad Al Suud; certainly Biden did strongly express the controlling of animal instincts, compared with his somewhat wilder opponent. He did pour out the sweet, tamed water to feed the people. Saturn, one of the descriptive stars in this mansion, is strong in his natal chart, so the positive nature of the mansion worked for him. As we can see here the mansion the progressed Moon is moving through will also provide guidelines on how to act, how to choose the most positive role in the mythical scenario of the mansion.

25. Al Sa'd – Akhbiya: 11.45 Pisces - 24.36 Pisces

Star: Sadalmelek (the Right Hand of Aquarius)

Arabic letter: Fa

Associated names: Lucky Star of Hidden Things/Planter

Planets and energies: Saturn/Mercury – Cultivation/feeding/growth

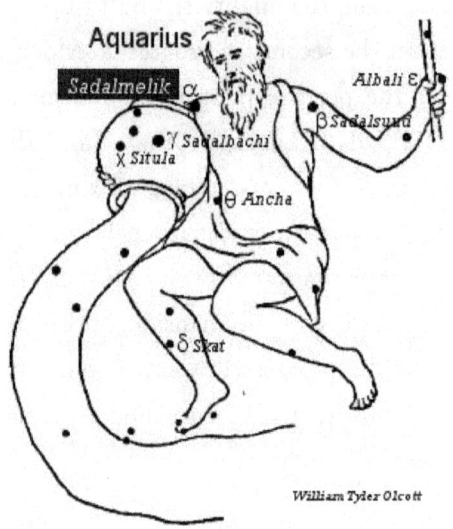

This twenty-fifth mansion is the third Aquarius mansion, so here all the themes of the purification of the desire Waters are found, the pouring out to feed others and the same mythological associations as in the previous two mansions. In Arabic the name means 'the Lucky Star of Hidden Things' and this sounds quite promising. In this third phase of the three Aquarian constellational zones, the focus is not on the left hand or the shoulder, but on the right hand holding the jug itself, where the whole process is taking place. The hidden things in the name refer to this; Aquarius can be associated with secrecy, this purification process cannot take place in public, so we have another emphasis here - it is less generous and public than the previous mansion, and tends to hold back more.

The 28 Mansions – Al Sa'd – Akhbiya

The descriptive star in this mansion is Sadalmelek which is translated as 'the Lucky One of the King', so the positive connotations seem to be repeated here. The planetary energies are again Saturn and Mercury underlining this process of purification; Saturn is connected to disciplining and purifying. It is important to realise that these symbolic explanations refer to the highest spiritual level, but concrete effects can take on many, many forms, also very banal or even evil ones. It all depends on the further context of the chart that we will see manifesting in the life, but every form of manifestation is *essentially* connected to the core mythology and all its symbolical ramifications.

As could be expected the keywords for this mansion are positive: planting, tilling, watering, ripening, increase. The only negative meaning has to do with love and marriage and this can be understood from the same keywords. It is all associated here with the slow growing of something planted but it is a very slow process which, also because of its agricultural associations, is very much a Saturn process. Naturally, most love relationships will grow over time but this is not quite the type of growth indicated by Saturn - the development of a relationship requires a bit more passion than agricultural Saturn has to offer. This is the reticent part as explained above, connecting with the emphasis on the jug and holding the Water contained in the jug. The less essential dignity Saturn has in the chart, the more this negative part will show.

The symbolic image does not leave too much to be explained; it is a man planting. Over time this will lead to results and fruits. The Arabic letter is Fa and its number is 80, connected to the doubled material 4, reflecting the slow growth, the element is Fire, associated with purification and distilling of the material dimension. This refers to the preparation of the Water to be poured out into the Fish's Mouth, a symbol of spiritual consciousness and knowledge of the most profound things. The creative step is connected to the level of The Angels, and its name is 'the Strong'. In the Vedic series there is no corresponding mansion.

In this mansion it is all about growth, gradual expansion, nurturing and bearing fruit, but it is not good for love and relationships.

A good example of how this mansion may work out in a life is the chart of Hugh Hefner, the founder of the Playboy Empire. The first thing to notice in this chart is the Sun, the essential masculine planet in its exaltation in Aries, so it thinks it is wonderful; this is the Playboy Sun and everything is there to give him pleasure. It is clear that this Sun exalting itself is important as the Part of the Moon, also called the Part of Hunger, is disposed by the Sun, so there is a hunger for this exalted masculine stuff - I wanna play! By antiscion the Moon, the essential female planet is in opposition with the Playboy Sun (as the two Luminaries' energies are involved the usual antiscial orb of two degrees can be expanded a bit). This is like an antiscial Full Moon, a tense connection between the archetypal masculine and the archetypal feminine energy in which the Sun dominates.

This Moon in its original position is on the powerful first magnitude star Achernar, which has a Jupiter nature and as the Mouth of the River is associated with pouring out, but also with stealing the solar chariot; it's exalted male stuff again. The two female planets, the Moon and Venus, are placed in the sixth house which is the turned twelfth of secrets, seen from the seventh of relationships - secret women - again, I wanna play. Aesthetic Venus is in its exaltation on the first magnitude star Deneb in the constellation the Swan, a very Venusian constellation. Whatever you think of it, it is not hard porn and it is certainly aesthetic in a way; exaltation tends to exaggerate, to become a bit rosy. Very interesting is this Uranus on the descendant - the primordial Sky-god who does not want to be limited and will try to escape castration by Saturn, only one partner, no way.

Mercury is key in this chart as it rules the most important houses, the first and the tenth, it is placed in a strong angular house and by antiscion (hidden things again) it is conjunct the ascendant. Mercury is the magazine planet; it is retrograde so it will not be mainstream, it is also conjunct the Part of Mars - the Part of Courage - and yes, what Hefner did when he started out was daring and he knew he would not be able to avoid going to court. The MC of the job conjuncts Betelgeuze, one of the main stars in Orion; the brute Hunter of animals and women alike, it is a star of great success. On the ascendant is Labrum, a star of fate associated with looking for higher beauty in this earthly dirt down here.

In this context Al Sad al Akhbiya, fits in perfectly. This water poured out for the people is refined water not salt, not hard porn water - leave that to Harry Flynt. It is made *acceptabl*e, and the mansion repeats the notion of hidden things found so clearly in the chart by the many active antiscia.

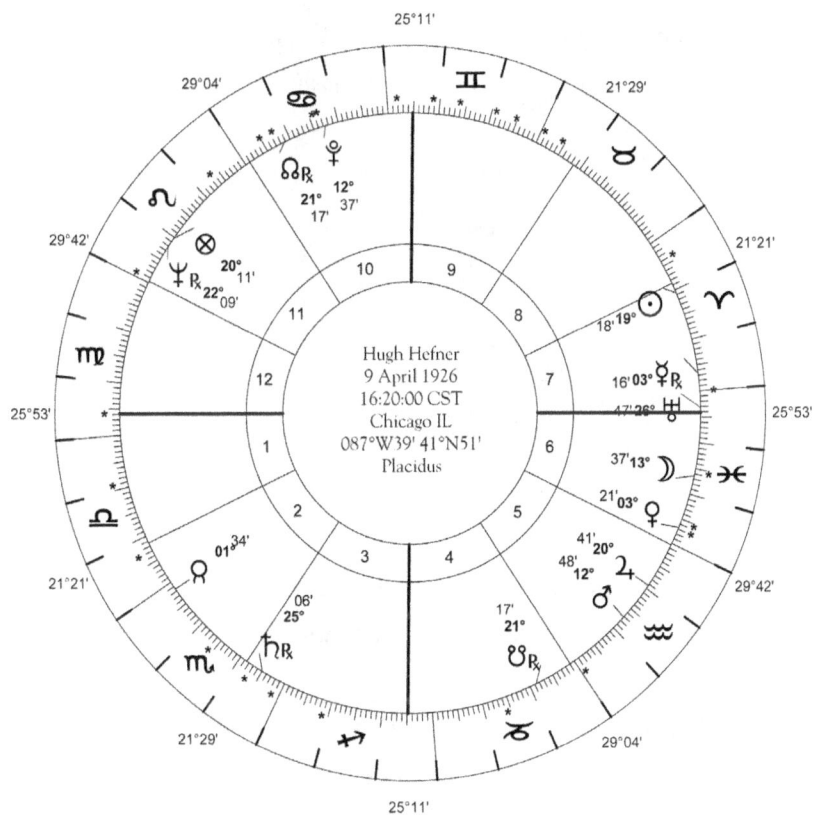

The Lunar Mansions Guide

Even the idea that this mansion harms relationships is to the point. Saturn, one the descriptive planetary energies only has weak Face essential dignity, it is not hard porn but that is all. The other descriptive energy Mercury, the magazine planet, is peregrine but it will be able to manifest strongly as it is placed in an angular house and in conjunction with the ascendant by antiscion.

---

26. Al Fargh al–Awwal: 24.36 Pisces – 7.27 Aries

Star: Markab (Pegasus)

Arabic letter: Ba

Associated names: The Horse's Wing/The Upper Spout of the Water-Bucket/The Beauty

Planets and energies: Mars/Mercury – Charm/love/attachment

In the twenty-sixth mansion Aquarius is left behind and we arrive in the last constellation of the cycle, Pisces. This immediately calls up questions: it is a bit mysterious that this mansion and the next one are said to be Pegasus mansions, as the three mansions closing the whole cycle all fall into the constellation of Pisces! So should we not regard them as Pisces mansions? Pisces as a constellation is about 40 degrees long and it could

The 28 Mansions – Al Fargh al–Awwal

easily contain three lunar mansions. As other constellations like Leo, Scorpio and even Aquarius are also connected to more than one mansion, there seems to be no principal reason that it would not be the same in the case of Pisces. So why do we have this Pegasus influence here?

On the level of the traditional images of the constellations in the sky, and that material is always our point of departure, it is clear. *Above* Pisces there is the constellation of Pegasus close to Andromeda. The Andromeda story is strongly connected with Pegasus, the flying horse on which rides the hero Perseus, who saves Andromeda from the Sea-monster. When Pegasus and Andromeda are projected into the zodiac, they fall in the zodiacal degrees occupied by these last three mansions, the twenty-sixth and the twenty-seventh Pegasus mansions - and the last one is said to be an Andromeda mansion. But *that* is not the point; the point is that the constellation of Pisces is much closer to the zodiac than Pegasus and Andromeda as it is a zodiacal constellation. Should it not have been preferred above the non-zodiacal constellations - Pegasus and Andromeda – which are further away?

It remains a bit of a mystery, but one of the possible reasons is that Pisces does not seem to have a very clear mythological story. It is said that the two Fishes are Venus and Cupid, who unexpectedly ran into Typhon and escaped by jumping into the water, after which two fishes saved them. This is the same story as Capricorn, where Pan escaped the threat of Typhon by changing from a goat into a fish and swimming off. In the Pisces story there is also this theme of changing into a 'fishy state', symbolically pointing at closing off one cycle to go to the next one on a higher spiritual level; the fish is a symbol of spiritual consciousness.

It seems though that things get a bit shaky at the end of the cycle, as there is also a lack of clarity in regard to the name. In Arabic the mansion is called 'Al Fargh Al Awwal' or 'Al Fargh Al Mukdim', said to mean 'the Upper Spout of the Water Bucket'. What on earth is a water bucket doing here? That sounds more like Aquarius, but the Water-bearer has been left behind. Another point is that the translation of the name *Awwal* is 'wing', while Al Farg refers to a horse - quite logically this is the horse's wing, which is exactly the focus point in this mansion of the Flying Horse. The mysterious Upper Spout maybe could refer in an indirect way to Pisces. Fishes are the kings of the desire waters, which here are kept in a bucket, controlled and safe. There seems to be a mixing of Pisces (controlled Water) and Pegasus (the Horse's Wing) themes here. Maybe we could see this mansion as a both a Pegasus and a Pisces mansion?

According to mythology the Flying Horse was born from the blood of Medusa, the monstrous woman with snakes as hair, after her decapitation by Perseus, the hero. This is logical symbolism; the decapitation of Medusa is the sacrifice of the desire nature, so when the horse gets wings its bondage to the earthly nature is broken. The horse's instinctive energies and driving powers are used now for higher things. It is also logical that after killing Medusa, Perseus rides through the skies on the back of Pegasus and saves Andromeda, symbol of the soul, from the Sea-Monster sent to devour her. The theme in this mansion is saving the soul by sacrificing the desire nature. The second part of the Pegasus story will be told in the next section on the second Pegasus mansion; that part is connected with dangerous over-confidence and a refusal to accept guidance. However, as this and the next mansion are both connected to Pegasus, each with a different emphasis, this basic mythical theme will to a certain extent play a role in both mansions.

The point of departure will be to see this mansion mainly as a Pegasus mansion and then its star would be Markab and the descriptive planets Mars and Mercury; Perseus riding Pegasus is a competent warrior. It may not come as a surprise with a view to the Perseus story that the keywords in this mansion are very positive: magnetism, appeal, connection, aid, sympathy, and love, as Perseus the hero saves Andromeda and marries her. Or maybe thinking of the Water bucket, the desire waters are successfully contained here and used to create an emotional connection. The symbolic image is a woman washing and combing her hair, which requires no explanation.

The Arabic letter in this mansion is Ba, its number is 2, symbolically material duality and division which is conquered here; its element is Air, indicating the escape from material bondage. The creative step is 'the astral world of the Jinn' or the Faeries, the astral beings living in the praeternatural world above matter, also called the subtle or imaginal world. The parallel Vedic mansion is interesting as this is also a Pegasus mansion, only with a clear emphasis on the darker sides of the myth, the rejection of guidance.

In this mansion it is all about love, relationship and connecting.

A good example of how this mansion may work out in a life is the chart of the French politician and Freemason Dominique Strauss-Kahn, who was also a university professor and the President of the International Monetary Fund. DSK, as his name is often abbreviated in France, was the socialist presidential candidate who might well have been able to beat right-wing Nicolas Sarkozy in the 2012 French elections.

However, in 2011 he was arrested in New York for sexual harassment of a chamber-maid in a hotel; he had to give up his IMF job so could not run for president any more. In the end, however, no reliable evidence for the accusations could be found and he was released. Later he was acccused of rape by another woman in France, but he was not convicted and again no evidence could be found in another case for the accusation that he had arranged prostitutes for sex parties. Despite many accusations DSK was never convicted. He still works as an international financial consultant and has a clean record. But it will be clear that this affair was one of the most important, maybe *the* most important, events in his life.

The Lunar Mansions Guide

The first thing we notice here is the power in this chart; DSK was hugely successful. Mars is Lord 10 in its domicile in the tenth house on the expansive North Node. That is very, very strong and it explains his IMF job and the political career. This is supported by Jupiter, right on the descendant, the planet of teachers, politics and knowledge is also on powerful first magnitude Altair, the main star in the Eagle of a Mars/Jupiter nature. Altair is associated with spreading knowledge, Jupiter is also Lord 9, the house associated with foreign countries and universities, so yes, the university professor is clearly indicated here.

Placement on the descendant makes a planet very strong, but it tends to remain a bit shaky as this is the house of the others opposing you, so it is not as completely at your disposal as it would have been on the

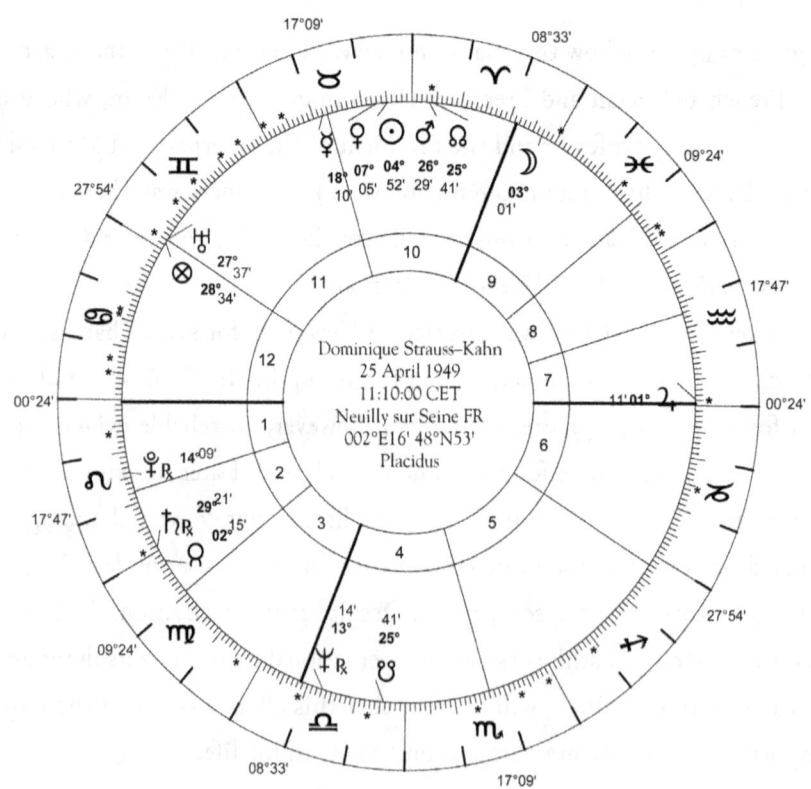

ascendant. In the tenth house of the job is a conjunction of the Sun/Lord 1 (DSK himself) and Venus Lord 11 (the fruits of your labours). Venus is not harmed much by this combustion as it is in its own sign, so the conjunction will work more like a positive mutual reception. It also shows the great importance of women as Venus is the general significator of women. Venus is placed on fierce Hamal, one of the Ram's Horns, associated with the story of brother and sister Phryxos and Helle. Helle is left behind as she falls into the sea, a good description of DSK's obsessive womanizing.

Saturn is Lord 7 of other people and relationships, and is retrograde, in its detriment on the powerful king star Regulus. Such an essentially weak Saturn on a very powerful star as Lord 7 shows no limitation or discipline in love, but also very powerful opponents. This Saturn is trine Mars Lord 10, a clear warning this could have a bad effect on his career. The Part of Fortune, his deepest hunger, is right on the cusp of the twelfth house of all the things God has forbidden; it is also on Betelgeuze, the arrogant hunter. Uranus, the sky-god and his unlimited potential is nearby. Saturn wants to castrate Uranus to discipline him and bring him to his senses, but the question is whether DSK is going to allow this.

Mars, the strong Lord 10, is also Lord 5 of sexuality and the Parts of Venus and Mars, the archetypical love couple, are conjunct in opposition with the Moon; a conjunction of parts shows a special dominant motive in the life. The emphasis on women is overwhelming in this chart as is the harm it may cause to his career. Saturn, Lord 7 of relationships, harms Lord 10, Venus is conjunct Lord 1 in mutual negative reception with Lord 10 of the job, and the conjunction of the Mars and Venus parts oppose the Moon. The mansion fits perfectly – remember, its image is a woman washing and combing her hair.

The planetary energies of Mars and Mercury are well-placed, so he will be able to manifest the potential of this mansion; it gave him his charisma and a powerful ability to attract, which is also applicable in his career. However, the other side of Pegasus is clearly also there, the fall from the horse as a consequence of over-confidence and rejecting guidance. It is interesting to note that in 2011 when this affair brought him down, his Moon was progressing through Al Haqa, the mansion of Orion, the proud hunter killed by the Scorpion.

---

27. Al Fargh al Thani: 7.27 Aries - 20.19 Aries

Star: Algenib (Pegasus)/Alpheratz (Andromeda)

Arabic letter: Mim

Associated names: The Second Horse/Lower Spout of the Water-Bucket/The Empty Vessel

Planets and energies: Mars/Mercury – Loss/danger/damage/decrease

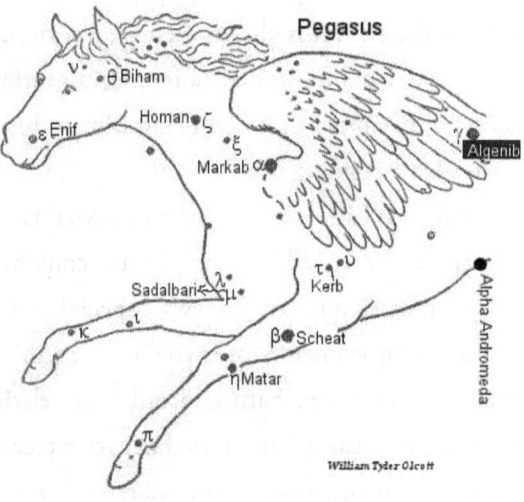

This is the second mansion attributed to Pegasus and its name is said to mean the Lower Spout of the Water-Bucket; the first Pegasus mansion was the Upper Spout. This difference suggests that in the first mansion the bucket is filled and in this mansion it is emptied. The name can also be translated as the Second Horse (Al Fargh being the horse) which seems to be very logical. The whole mythological story of the Flying Horse also

The 28 Mansions – Al Fargh al Thani

applies in this mansion, and the central theme is self-will, not accepting any guidance, but there isn't a lot of connection made here as in this mansion the more destructive part of the Pegasus story dominates.

In the first part of the myth it is the hero Perseus who rides Pegasus, born out of the blood of Medusa, the horrible Gorgon with snakes as hair who was decapitated by him. The birth of the Flying Horse is a result of the sacrifice of the desire nature symbolised by the snakes on Medusa's head. After killing Medusa Perseus flies off on Pegasus, saves Andromeda, symbol of the soul, from the Seamonster and marries her. There is a very positive side to this first part of the Pegasus story but it continues with another rider, Bellerophon and his story is not nice. Bellerophon, riding on Pegasus, first killed the Chimaera, a hideous creature part lion (lust for power), part snake (desire) and part goat (earth), so a symbol of totally chaotic forces. He did this by throwing a chunk of lead in its mouth. Lead is the metal of Saturn, so this refers to discipline.

After this victory however, Bellerophon becomes over-confident and decides to fly to the world of the gods on Mount Olympus. This is not allowed; you cannot enter the divine world on your own initiative, it has to be given to you by grace, so you can't just force your way in. As a result Zeus was not amused and sent a fly that stung Pegasus; consequently Bellerophon fell to earth from Pegasus and spent the remainder of his life crippled, blind and lonely. This myth is about pride and over-confidence, lack of respect for limitations, and going where you are not supposed to go. We can see that in DSK's case these Pegasus themes also played a role; it is, after all, about the same myth in both mansions.

The descriptive star here is Algenib, which like Markab is a star on the wing of the Flying Horse; the planetary energies here are Mars and Mercury, battle and dexterity, but also pragmatism. It may not come as a surprise that the keywords are negative in this second mansion, emphasising Bellerophon's fall: loss, emptying, lack of energy, misfortune, self-destruction and harm. The symbolic image does not require much explanation; it is a

The Lunar Mansions Guide

winged man holding an empty perforated vessel, clearly associated with the Lower Spout in the mansion's name, by which the vessel is emptied.

The Arabic letter is Mim, its number is 40, the symbol of matter into which Bellerophon fell back to earth. Its element is Fire, and it is said to symbolise the dualistic relationship between material forces and divine power, which indeed seems to be the core mythological issue here (flying to Mount Olympus). The creative step is 'the phase of man', also called 'He who unites man' as the microcosm contains everything - the earthly and the divine.

It's interesting to note that in the Vedic series of lunar mansions there are also two Pegasus mansions, one of which has a more positive meaning and one a more negative meaning - so we have the same split into two parts of the myth. However, the Vedic version has the first mansion as the more negative one in which self-will dominates and the second one as the more positive one, so just the other way around.

In this mansion it is all about obstacles, friction, loss and rejection of guidance.

A good example of how this mansion may work out in a life is the natal chart of American actress Angelina Jolie, who became world-famous as a female action hero in the *Tomb Raider* films. What strikes the eye in her chart are the four planets around the two most important angles, the ascendant and the MC. This indicates a lot of power to manifest in the world, a high chance of success. Astrologically, success can be given in several ways, but having many angular planets is certainly one of the more important indications for some special achievements.

On the ascendant is Venus, the planet of beauty and the arts, both of which certainly apply in this case. Venus on the ascendant is in mundane square with Jupiter, right on the MC. The connection with Jupiter is not bad for this Venus; it will only enlarge its power to manifest in the world.

Mars is Lord 10 of the profession, and essentially very strong in its own sign, so combined with Venus on the ascendant the female action hero is clearly indicated here. The strong Mars is important in the chart as it also disposes two other planets around the MC, the Moon and Jupiter. It is a very special Mars as its speed is considerably higher than average; it is placed in Aries, the sign of cardinal fast-moving Fire and it is conjunct the Part of Mars! This is an extremely martial Mars; Jolie is not a tomb raider by accident. Mars is also ruler of the fifth house of creativity, a channel for a lot of energy.

It is also interesting to note that Venus, the planet of the feminine, on the ascendant is conjunct the South Node by antiscion. The South Node takes things away and requires a sacrifice. This points to the fact that her roles tend to be very masculine, but it has manifested on another level too. Angelina Jolie decided to have her breasts amputated as according to her doctors there was a high chance she would develop breast cancer in the long run, just like her mother. Venus can be associated with female organs and the sign of Cancer is anatomically connected to the breast. Jupiter, strong on the MC, is Lord 6 of illness and general significator of growths, and it squares Saturn in its detriment also in Cancer; a Saturn in detriment has lost all power to limit. This Jupiter/Lord 6 is also in mundane square with Venus on the ascendant, so there are clear indications for these medical problems; the chart seems to confirm the doctors' fears.

The Moon is Lord 1, Angelina Jolie in her life situation, and it is on the MC within the traditional 5° orb for cusps. The Moon is disposed by and conjunct Lord 10, not only the career but also the mother, as she indeed had a very good relationship with her mother. Venus is Lord 4, the father, conjunct the painful South Node by antiscion, and it can be seen that her relationship with her father was more difficult. The Moon/Lord 1 in Aries is in the sign where Venus has its detriment, so she was not very fond of him. Mars nearby is the mother and Mars is in mutual negative reception with Venus/Lord 4 the father. The receptions reflect these tense family relationships.

The Moon/Lord 1 is also in the sign where Saturn has its fall; Saturn is Lord 7, indicating important themes in relationships. She tends to harm relationships because she does not like the limiting disciplining energy they bring, further destabilizing Lord 7 which is very weak as it is in its fall. As there are four planets in the chart working against Lord 7, it comes as no surprise that she has divorced three times. Lord 7 of relationships is also on the Gemini star Wasat, with a purely Saturnian nature, and it is placed in the twelfth house of isolation, which does not give stability in marriage.

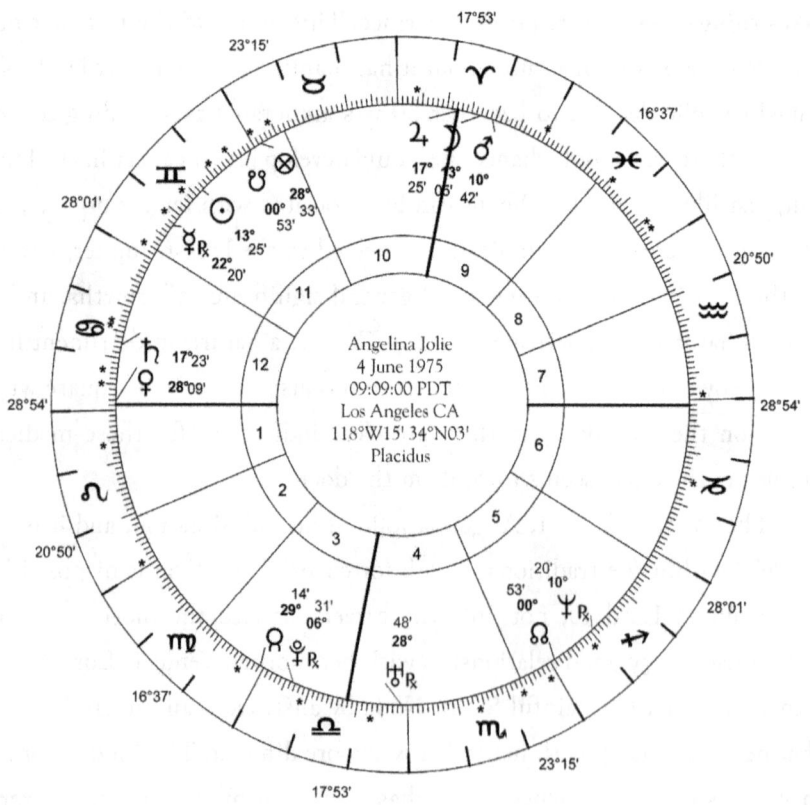

The second Pegasus mansion fits in well as it gives a strong self-will and the rejection of guidance. Let us say this is not a mansion of temperance, and that also works out in relationships. Her role as Laura Croft in *Tomb Raider,* so essential for her career, was extremely violent; Bellerophon, the rider of Pegasus, also fought a monster just as Jolie did in this movie. It will be clear from this example that keywords should not be taken literally as she is of course extremely successful. Mars and Mercury, the planets describing this mansion, are both very strong in her chart so, despite the fact that we can recognize the myth's problematic themes, it will not work out in a purely negative way for her.

---

28. Al Batn al Hut: 20.19 Aries - 3.11 Taurus

Star: Mirach (Alrisha/Al Pherg)

Arabic letter: Waw

Associated names: The Fishes' Belly

Planets and energies: Venus (Saturn/Jupiter) – Conclusion/connection/ending of the cycle/assembling/harvesting.

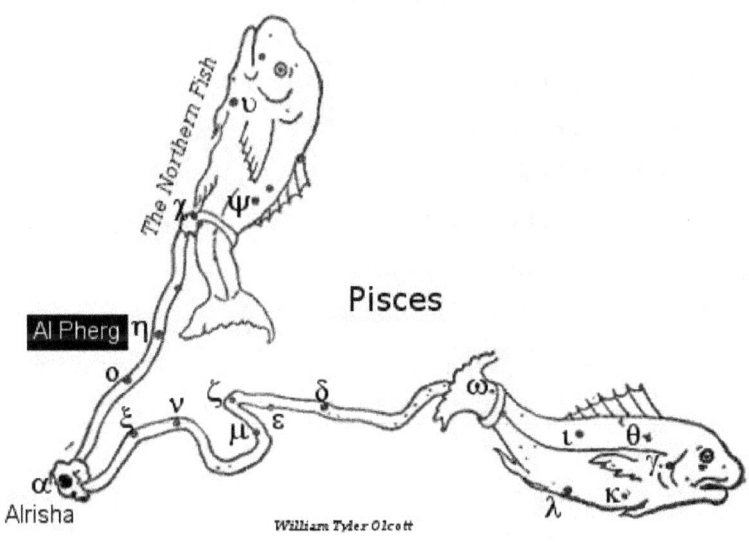

In this twenty-eighth mansion the cycle is closed and everything seems to be clear, and just as in the solar zodiac, it is Pisces that marks this ending. In Pisces the vertical Northern Fish and the horizontal Southern Fish are tied together by the famous cord. This is why the cycle ends here - the two Fishes represent the polar forces, Yang and Yin, masculine and feminine, Sulphur and Mercury that keep the world going, and when they unite the world ends. That is also the reason why the only star in Pisces of direct practical relevance in astrology (Al Pherg) is known as a star of fate; the cycle ends and soon there will be a new start.

The name for this mansion is also quite clear, Batn Al Hut, meaning the Fishes' Belly. The second mansion Al Butain has the same linguistic root, and it translates from Arabic as 'the Small Belly' to distinguish it from the big belly here. But then again there is confusion, like there is in the two previous mansions. This mansion falls in the constellation of Pisces but the texts don't attribute it to Pisces despite its name and its image (which is also a fish, see below). It is said to be associated with Andromeda, a constellation that also falls into these longitudinal degrees but is much further away from the zodiac.

So the same problem as in the two previous mansions is repeated. They are associated with the Pegasus constellation, also further away from the zodiac than Pisces. In the two previous mansions the traditional texts were followed and the mansions were delineated as parts of Pegasus with their associated mythical themes. In this case following the texts and seeing this last mansion as an Andromeda mansion seems a bit more problematic as there are so many indications that this mansion is connected to the Fishes. It will be seen as a Pisces mansion although the Andromeda themes will be kept in mind. The descriptive stars and planets associated with Pisces are bracketed above, as according to the old texts the star Mirach and the planet Venus describe this mansion.

So if the Pisces constellation is taken as the foundation for understanding the mansion, the descriptive stars are Al Pherg and Al Risha, marking the

The 28 Mansions – Al Batn al Hut

point where the two lines are connected and it would give a good picture of what this mansion is about. The story of Venus and Cupid, both strongly connected to love, escaping from Typhon by jumping into the water and being saved by Fishes is also relevant as there is the idea of bringing two polar opposites (the Northern and the Southern Fish) together, the change to another state and the end of a cycle. Andromeda would introduce the theme of the princess chained to the island, threatened by the Sea Monster and saved by Perseus, who marries her, as told in the previous chapter. So both perspectives share the theme of bringing together.

The keywords given in the texts are very logical from the Pisces perspective: relationship, completion, bonding, assembling, love, finalisation. It will be clear that this mansion is also good for love; to this might be added the idea of waiting for the new cycle to start in a phase of preparation and processing all the experiences of the whole cycle. The symbolic image could not be clearer: it is a fish, the Arabic letter is Waw, connected to the Air element, the number is 6, the double 3 which is the number of the spirit. So this mirrors the two fishes, the fish is very much a symbol of spirituality.

The letter Waw is said to represent the mystical promise of the ascent to God, so there we have the closing of the cycle and the unity with the divine. It refers to the perfect human being, an indication of connecting all forces, and another illustration of Pisces at the end of the cycle. The creative step is called 'the hierarchisation of the degrees of Existence, not their manifestation', or 'He who elevates by degrees'. There is the idea of collecting everything and giving everything its appropriate place as a preparation for the next cycle to start in Aries. The parallel Vedic mansion gives the same idea of connection and adds the idea of an association with time which is logical as time ends here, this is the end of the cycle.

In this mansion it is all about collecting, bringing together, ending a cycle, preparation for the new cycle, reaping; it also good for love and marriage.

A good example of how this mansion may work out in a life is the chart of the eternal Prince of Wales, Charles of Windsor; now there is someone waiting for a new cycle! The first thing we notice in his chart explains this situation; the Moon is high in the chart, totally dominating it, and everything else is below the horizon. This Moon has just entered its exaltation in Taurus and it feels great there. Taurus is fixed Earth, the Moon has another 29° of Taurus to go, so it will stay there forever. This Moon is of course his mother as the Moon is the general significator of mothers and it is placed in the tenth house of mothers.

Again the planetary parts indicate very specific and important individual motives, as the antiscion of the Part of the Sun, the essence of the solar royal energy, opposes this Moon. He can't be king because of his mother being up there - the Solar Part's antiscion is also conjunct the South Node, the point where things are withheld! On top of that the Part of Mercury, also called Despair, opposes Mars, Lord 10 of the profession. Praesepe, the Empty Crib is found on the ascendant; the king-child is not in the place where it should be, which repeats what the Solar Part has to say. This nebulous heap of stars tends to create chaos and fragmentation, so the way to prevent this is not to let yourself be distracted and just carry on doing what your main task is.

Also noticeable is Venus, strong in its domicile and in an angular house, the fourth house of the family, the dynasty. Now on one level this is certainly Diana, and it is clearly indicated that this Venus will not be good for him - not only by chaotic Neptune nearby but also by the receptions. Venus in Libra will harm the ruler of the opposite sign, Mars/Lord 10; it will harm his public position, and it will harm the planet in exaltation in the opposite sign to the Sun, not only the significator of kings but also Lord 1, Charles himself. The Sun/Lord 1 is in the sign of Scorpio where Venus has its detriment, so the Sun also harms Venus; this is a mutual negative reception, and any competent astrologer would have told the Prince of Wales not to get involved with very Venus-like girls like Diana. Although they may look very nice and may even be very nice, this is certainly not good for him.

The three essentially strong planets in his chart, the Moon, Venus and Jupiter, show the most important women in his life: his mother, Diana and Camilla. Camilla is Jupiter, strong in its own sign of Sagittarius in the fifth house of pleasure, but in the second sign on the house and placed in the last degree of the sign, showing she will be late, almost too late; there are only seven minutes left before she enters her fall. Jupiter is better for him than Venus, as the Great Benefic is not in any strong negative reception

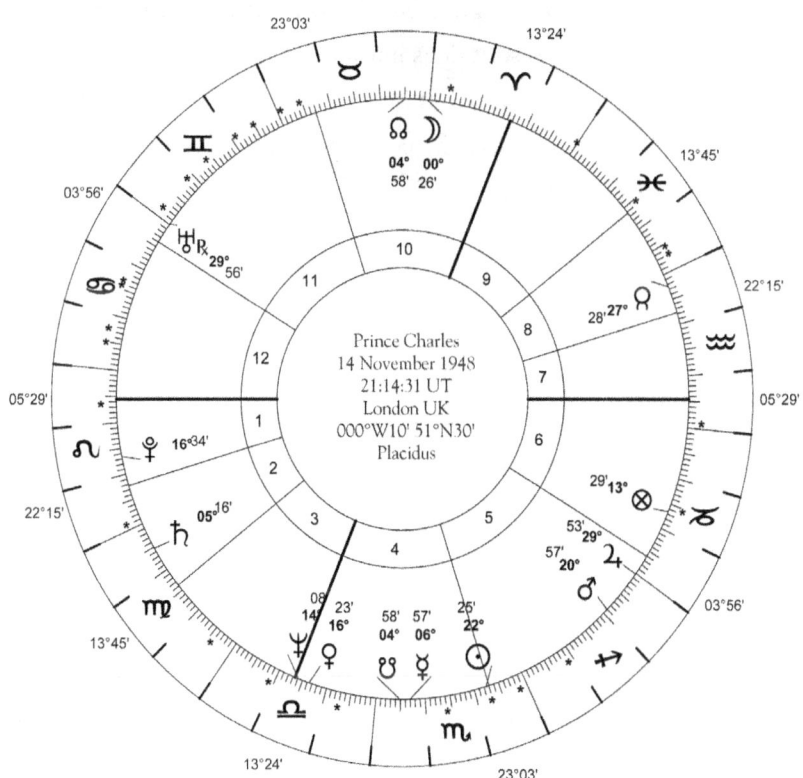

with the Sun or Lord 10 of the profession like Venus. Of course, Saturn Lord 7 says something about what is going on in relationships in general and this Saturn without any dignity will manifest its negative sides; it is this royal family straitjacket that makes many things impossible.

The last mansion of the cycle certainly fits in with all this. The Moon is placed a few degrees before the start of the new cycle in Al Sharatain, the first Aries mansion, almost visible from here, where the new fresh flame will be lit. This gives us the picture of someone in the waiting room, just before the beginning, and as the mansion is the central story in the life, also on a concrete level, it is clear: he has been waiting all his life, always so close. The idea of connecting the two basic polarities as a central theme in the mansion is also clear; the whole Diana drama is the main event in his life. This mansion is said to be as good for love and marriage as it is about connections of the polar energies, but there is also the association with moving to the next phase, so it does not mean that every relationship will be good. The mansion will work out in the context of the rest of the chart. This is the Pisces mythological theme of change to a new level caused by adverse unexpected circumstances.

APPENDIX A

Comparing the Arabian and the Vedic mansions - Boundaries in tropical degrees for 2000

Below are given:

The *tropical* boundaries of the 28 Western mansions, the constellational nature of the parallel 27 Vedic mansions, the *tropical* boundaries of the Vedic mansions and the traditional medical/anatomical associations of the Vedic mansions. Vedic mansions were calculated according to the Lahiri ayanamsha (start of the mansion cycle opposite Spica) for the year 2000.

The medical/physical associations supposed to be indicating extra sensitive body parts are also valid for the Vedic mansions.

Western (28)	Vedic (27)	Physical
1. Aries Horns 3.11-16.02 Tau	Aries 1 23.50 Ar-7.10 Tau	Knee, feet
2. Aries Hindpart 16.02-28.53 Tau	Aries 2 7.10-20.30 Tau	Head, feet
3. Taurus Pleiads 28.53 Tau-11.45 Gem	Pleiades 20.30 Tau-3.50 Gem	Hips, head, groin
4. Taurus Eye 11.45-24.36 Gem	Taurus 3.50-17.10 Gem	Shin, calf
5. Orion Head 24.36 Gem-7.28 Can	Orion 1 17.10 Gem-0.30 Can	Many pediatric diseases
6. Gemini Pollux's Foot 7.28-20.20 Can	Orion 2 0.30 Can-13.50 Can	Eyes, head
7. Gemini Castor's Head 20.20 Can- 3.11 Leo	Gemini 13.50-27.10 Can	Lungs, TB
8. Cancer Cancer Heart 3.11-16.02 Leo	Cancer 27.10 Can-10.30 Leo	Face mole
9. Leo Eyes 16.02-28.54 Leo	Hydra 10.30-23.50 Leo	Joints, ears, nails

The Lunar Mansions Guide

Western (28)	Vedic (27)	Physical
10. Leo Head 28.54 Leo-11.45 Vir	Leo 1 23.50 Leo-7.10 Vir	Lungs
11. Leo Back 11.45-24.36 Vir	Leo 2 7.10-20.30 Vir	Lips, hands, sex organs
12. Leo Tail 24.36 Vir-7.28 Lib	Leo 3 20.30 Vir-3.50 Lib	As above
13. Virgo Wings 7.28-20.19 Libra	Crow 3.50 -17.10 Lib	Hands, fingers, heart
14. Virgo Ear 20.19 Lib-3.10 Sco	Virgo 17.10 Lib-0.30 Sco	Neck, head, bladder
15. Maagd Robe 3.10-16.02 Sco	Boötes 0.30-13.50 Sco	Breast, intestines
16. Libra Scorpion's Claw 16.02-28.53 Sco	Scales 13.50-27.10 Sco	Breast, arms
17. Scorpion Head 28.53 Sco-11.44 Sag	Scorpion 1 27.10 Sco-10.30 Sag	Stomach, belly
18. Scorpion Heart 11.44 -24.36 Sag	Scorpion 2 10.30-23.50 Sag	Neck, torso
19. Scorpion Tail 24.36 Sag-7.28 Cap	Scorpion 3 23.50 Sag-7.10 Cap	Torso, feet, joints
20. Sagittarius Arrow 7.28-20.19 Cap	Sagittarius 1 7.10-20.30 Cap	Back, Bladder
21. Sagittarius Hindpart 20.10 Cap-3.11 Aq	Sagittarius 2 20.30 Cap-3.50 Aq	Waist
22. Capricorn Eye 3.11-16.03 Aq	Eagle 3.50-17.10-Aq	Ears, skin sex organs
23. Aquarius Left hand 16.03-28.53 Aq	Delphin 17.10 Aq-0.30 Pis	Anus, back
24. Aquarius Shoulder 28.53 Aq-11.45 Pis	Aquarius 0.30 -13.50 Pis	Jaws, right thigh
25. Aquarius Right Hand 11.45-24.36 Pis	Pegasus 1 13.50-27.10 Pisces	Left thigh, feet
26. Pegasus Wing 24.36 Pis-7.27 Ar	Pegasus 2 27.10 Pis-10.30 Ar	Shin-bone
27. Pegasus Wing Tip 7.27-20.19 Ar	Pisces 10.30 -23.50 Ar	Intestines, feet, ankle
28. Pisces Fish's Belly 20.19 Ar-3.11 Tau		

APPENDIX A

The systems are similar, but the Arabian-Western system follows the zodiacal constellations more closely, only the Arabic mansions No. 5 (Orion) and No. 26/27 (Pegasus) are extra-zodiacal, although there remains some doubt about No. 28 (is it really Andromeda or is it Pisces?).

The Vedic system has two times Orion, the Hydra, the Crow, Boötes, the Delphin, the Eagle and two times Pegasus, so nine extra-zodiacal mansions, a third of the mansions! In the Vedic system Capricorn has no mansion. The stronger emphasis on the visible constellation is appropriate for the Vedic system with its starting-point in a visible star.

The main difference is that the Vedic series has 27 instead of 28 mansions and its starting-point is not given by the first star in the Aries constellation but by the star Revati in the middle of the Pisces constellation (opposite Spica).

Appendix B

The precession and the illusion of the Age of Aquarius

The precession movement is generally not understood clearly enough in astrology, which is unfortunate as this incomplete understanding has given rise to influential, though illusory ideas like that of the Age of Aquarius. On top of that, a clear grasp of the precession is also necessary to use the fixed stars in an effective and correct way. The precession is astrologically a fundamental phenomenon and the ancient model of the spheres will provide the right perspective on what it really is.

The precession is the very slow displacement of the vernal equinox point measured against the background of the fixed stars. The Vernal Equinox Point (VP) moves at a speed of about one degree in 72 years and the result is that the stars the VP falls on change as the ages go by. This movement of the VP, which is by definition 0° Aries in the tropical zodiac used in the West, is however only apparent as the zodiac, also by definition, cannot move at all.

In order to clarify this idea in a way which views things from a cosmological perspective and not from a more superficial material or astronomical level, it is necessary to explain the ancient all-important model of the spheres. It was this model that also provided the background to Dante's masterpiece the *Commedia Divina*, so we are in very good company here. The model of the spheres has as its centre the earth which is surrounded by concentric circles, the first seven of which are the spheres of the planets; the Moon of course occupies the first sphere and Saturn the seventh. It is important to see the model in motion; each sphere turns around within the sphere immediately above it like a wheel inside a bigger wheel.

Schema huius præmissæ diuisionis Sphærarum.

This image is illuminating because the eighth sphere above Saturn, in which we find the fixed stars as well as the lunar mansions, is turning around *within* the sphere of the zodiac. In this model the stars really transit the signs just like the planets and in the same direction as the planets, but at a much slower pace. Also the outer planets find their proper places in the model in this sphere; Oeranus, Poseidon and Hades can be seen and treated as potent 'star-like' factors. The zodiac which constitutes the ninth sphere, directly above the fixed stars, does not move - it is the divine cosmic blueprint which will remain in place until the End of Time.

So it is this boundary between the eighth sphere of the fixed stars, the 'Firmamentum' and the ninth sphere of the zodiac the 'Crystallinum' (that which is crystalised, so never changes), which is so interesting. The eighth sphere of the fixed stars is visible to the eye and the ninth sphere of the zodiac is not, illustrating that the signs of the zodiac and the constellations we can see are of a very different nature. The constellation of Aries is not the same thing as the sign of Aries, and although there are relationships between the Aries constellation and the Aries sign, they are only similar, not identical. They could be seen as cousins - my cousin is close family but he is not me. The failure to see the fundamental difference between my cousin and me has led to some persistent errors in astrology, which are harmful because they tend to veil the truth about our modern times. The first among these is the Age of Aquarius.

The simple version of the Aquarius Age

The idea that we are entering some new age, which of course will be better than the backward Christian times we are leaving behind, has become a popular belief. As reactions to the ending of the Maya calendar in 2012 have shown, the idea of some new age dawning has become deeply rooted in many people's minds, not just those of astrologers. This is not the place to go into the differences between the ideas of the New Age and the Age of Aquarius; it is sufficient to know that in the popular mind and also in that of many astrologers, these ideas are very much connected. This may not be justified, nevertheless it is often seen this way and it is taught by many astrologers to their students.

In most cases this concerns the idea that the VP is now moving into the constellation/sign of Aquarius, which is said to mean that we are gradually leaving the Christian era of Pisces. There are no sound astrological arguments for this idea. It cannot be determined where the VP is exactly as it is moving not through the signs but through the constellations. However, the constellations have no clear boundaries like signs, and as

Appendix B

there is no such thing as a clear constellational 'cusp', it is impossible to say when the Age of Aquarius will start.

This is not a detail; it is unclear to such an extent that in articles and books about the Aquarian Age widely differing dates are mentioned from 1762 to 3042, illustrating the whole problem. Apart from this, there is another problem for the Age of Pisces as even without knowing exact boundaries, it would clearly be much, much longer than, for example, the Age of Aries or Cancer as we don't have 12 Ages of more or less equal duration. The Aries and Cancer constellations are much shorter than Pisces or Scorpio, for example. This seriously undermines the whole idea of 12 Ages connected to 12 signs; it cannot be so that one Age continues for more than 3000 years and another Age will only last less than a 1000. This and the lack of clarity about the constellational boundaries means that the simple version is astrologically untenable and it can be forgotten. It is founded on the confusion of the eighth and ninth spheres as it attempts to treat constellations as a kind of signs.

The sophisticated version of the Ages model

To solve this problem a sophisticated version was proposed which at first glance at least, has its attractive sides. This version was discussed by Robert Hand in an article in his book *Essays on Astrology* (Whitford Press 1982) and it is based on the chapters 6-9 in *Aeon*, a book on the Age of Pisces written by Carl Gustav Jung, who else? In this book Jung launched the idea of the *morphomaton*, a constellation in astrological terms which is worked out by Hand in a more detailed way. Jung, and Hand following him, look at the stars on the VP in a certain epoch and these stars' constellations are said to show the Age the world is in. This concerns the positions of the stars in the zodiacal constellations projected into the zodiac, which is common practice in astrology and correct.

The advantage compared to the simple model is that we now have clearer timing; when 0° Aries falls on a star in Pisces for the *first time*, the Piscean Age begins, this is in 111 BC. This more or less indicates the beginnings of Christianity, and further historical events are said to be explained by the stars and parts of Pisces moving over the VP. The first Eastern Fish is associated with the dominance of the Catholic Church, but in 1351 the VP is mid-way through Pisces and indeed this indicates, again roughly, the great turning-point in European history, the Renaissance. So this seems to work to a certain extent as regards the history of Christianity, only the problem is that the other historical events Hand mentioned in support of this model, are not very convincing at all. To get a clear picture of this idea refer to the spheres' model discussed above; it concerns stars moving over 0° Aries. You can conceive of the stars as a kind of planet going through the zodiac as the spheres' model shows. And yes, according to Jung's model, we are still in the middle of the Age of Pisces, and the Aquarian Age will start not until 2813, although he himself also makes rather confusing statements contradicting this. Consistency is a weak point in all of Jung's writings.

Technical problems

Despite the apparent advantages of the Jungian model of the morphomaton, as presented by Hand, great problems arise if it is critically and logically scrutinized. The first problem is its technical inconsistency, the second problem is that it also leads to Ages of very different durations and the third most serious problem is the interpretation of the Second Fish in Pisces as the Antichrist. The technical problem is that this model is principally based on the interpretation of the star 'transiting' the VP and its constellation. The nature of this constellation is said to give the nature of the epoch, and for Pisces it seems to work to a certain extent at least. But

Appendix B

if the idea is theoretically sound, it should work for other constellations and their associated Ages or epochs as well.

We get into trouble almost immediately if we try this. For example, the boundary between Aquarius and Capricorn cannot be found, so we are back at the problem in the simple model. When the last, most western star of Aquarius, *eta Aquarii,* is projected onto the zodiac it falls mid-way through Capricorn, but the first star of Capricorn is found much further east in the direction of the main body of Aquarius. So where/when does the Age of Capricorn start? The only way to get a clear boundary – a 'constellational cusp' - would be to ignore the part of Aquarius stretching out parallel to Capricorn on which *eta Aquarii* is placed. But this would of course be unthinkable. If we look further, the problems get worse, for example between the Capricorn and Sagittarius constellations there is a gap where there are no stars projected from zodiacal constellations.

This gap does, however, contain stars of the Eagle; does this mean there is an intermediate Age of the Eagle? You cannot say Eagle stars do not count because they are too far off, as some of the stars in Pisces that Jung and Hand make part of their system are further away from the zodiac than the Eagle stars. And it gets worse than this because what are we to make of the fact that the Snake-Bearer is in the zodiac? (The Aries and Sagittarius constellations are not!) Does this point to a possible short Age of the Snake-Bearer? The answer would be yes if the logical principle of the Jungian morphomaton model is consistently followed. What's more, the problem of Ages of very different durations is not solved in this model; the Age of Pisces would still be almost three times longer that the Age of Aries. Again this must be roughly estimated as we have problematic boundaries in many constellations here too.

This constitutes a definitive death-blow. The technical inconsistencies are insurmountable and the problem can only be solved by discarding all logic and consistency. Even if you decide to exclude all non-zodiacal constellations from the model, which would be a questionable thing to do in a model based on visible constellations, still the problem of unclear boundaries and unequal durations cannot be solved. But this is not all: there are even more serious problems in the symbolic interpretation of Pisces.

The Antichrist?

In developing this model of the Ages Robert Hand followed Jung, always a point of departure which calls for vigilance. The basis is that Jung divides Pisces into two Fishes, but he sees the first Fish as Christ and the second Fish as the Antichrist. So when stars in the Christ fish are on the VP we have the reign of Catholicism and if the stars in the second Fish are on the VP – as they are now – Christianity is over. This is not a very a plausible idea. In Christian symbolism the Antichrist is not Christ's dark brother or mirror image, he is a counterfeit Christ of a totally inferior order. He is a satanic manifestation in human form and Christ, the Son of God, is not exactly on the same level as the damned Angel of Dawn. It is very unlikely that the second Fish would symbolise the Antichrist; a fish is a symbol of divine consciousness, so it cannot be something of a sinister nature. The correct symbol for a demonic energy is a snake or a dragon as is shown clearly in the first book of the Bible, and in a lot of other traditional imagery.

It is interesting to cite what Hand writes about this:"The new order (of Antichrist – OH) is however not at all bad. The energy of the Antichrist is not any more intrinsically evil than that of what we have called the "Christ". Now this is a weird thing to say. The Antichrist IS, as a symbolic figure, a direct manifestation of the Evil One. What was young Robbie Hand doing when all the kids went to Sunday school? Maybe he has changed his views in the meantime. The whole formulation is not only a bit strange, it even sounds frightening. If I had a choice I would very much prefer the order

Appendix B

of Christ above an inevitable, 'new order' of Satan, and I am sure you would too.

This statement was directly inspired by Carl Gustav Jung and leads to some interesting observations. It is well-known that Jung disliked Christianity because of its central sacrificial nature and saw himself as a 'prophetic' mind bringing in the new religion of analytical psychology to replace it. In fact he tried to use the precession to get cosmic support for his project; to suggest the era of the first Fish of Christianity was over in his model, and the time for the Second Fish of Antichrist-Jungianism had come. Not only is the symbolism unlikely, but Jung had clear political motives which further disqualify his interpretations. It is always a good idea to read Jung critically as there is a tendency in his writings to give symbols creative meanings in order to make them fit his own particular ideas, ideologies, and prejudices. Some of his writing may be interesting, but there is no reason at all to see the man as the kind of prophet he pretended to be. He is wrong on too many points.

The conclusion can only be that neither the simple nor the sophisticated Jungian morphomaton model work well enough. There is no Age of Aquarius, nor an Age of Pisces, or any other Age attributed to a sign. There cannot be some New Age dawning in which we will all be spiritually liberated and in which astrology is broadly accepted again; it is mainly a politically motivated illusion for which there is no astrological evidence. It is based on a persistent confusion of the constellations with the signs in some form, on mistaking me for my cousin. You cannot force the more fluid overlapping constellations into the rigid mould of 12 signs; they just don't fit in. It must be accepted that we cannot determine exactly where we are in terms of precession.

And we don't need the precession for that, for the undeniably profound changes in our times are explained clearly and objectively by the cycles of the Great Conjunctions of Saturn and Jupiter as they have always been used in traditional mundane astrology. This cycle entering the

Air Triplicity now explains all the massive Air processes we see around us, like mass migration (and tourism!) globalisation and the extremely rapid developments in information/robot technology. Air is movement, knowledge, connection and communication. As for the nature of our times in a still wider time perspective, that is another story, but that story has nothing to do with a supposed Age of Aquarius, an untenable idea which only veils what is really going on.

At the most profound level the precession is a symbolic expression of the 'law of non-repetition' as explained by Sufi-master Ibn al-Arabi, the 'Shaykh al-Akbar', in the little jewel of a book written by Titus Burckhardt on his 'mystical astrology'. Nothing ever exactly repeats itself, as the divine creativity is infinite and inexhaustible, so the astrological model can never become a closed system. Even if after a very long time a certain constellation of planets should occur again, the stars are in totally different places because of the precession, creating a new unique moment. Everything is always opened up towards the divine, which can be seen in the model of the spheres, as the Empyreum embracing all the other spheres. That is why it is called *Habitaculum Dei*, the place where God lives.

Appendix C

Seven Pillars of Wisdom – The Planetary Parts

Planetary Parts represent the pure essences of the planetary energies so the Part of the Moon, better known as the Pars Fortunae, is the concentrated lunar energy with all its possible connotations. Formulas of calculation are always the same in diurnal and nocurnal charts.

Moon-Pars Fortunae/PF the part of fortune, of hunger, the lunar ascendant: Asc + Moon − Sun

Sun – Pars Solis/PS the part of abundance, the spirit or the future: Asc + Sun− Moon

Venus the part of (idealising) love, extra abundance − the unity essence: Asc + PS − PF

Mercury the part of despair, the necessity of choice, 'you can't have it all' extra hunger: Asc + PF-PS

Mars the part of courage, greatness of the soul, fighting for more than your direct interests: Asc + PF-Mars

Jupiter the part of victory and help from above: Asc + Jup − PS

Saturn the part of imprisonment and escape: Asc + PF − Sat

The formula of the Part of Mercury repeats the formula of the Part of Fortune only with the Parts of the Sun and the Moon instead of the Sun and the Moon themselves and it can be seen as a concentrated PoF, so as the part of unsatisfiable hunger. Mercury is despair because it divides everything into earthly detail.

The same applies to the Part of the Sun/Abundance and the Part of Venus (this part would be seen be extra abundance, because Venus unites everything).

Interpretation (the Parts work out in concrete but also in more psychological and spiritual ways):

If the Parts conjunct/oppose planets or other astrological factors with a small orb (2°), this shows a very important contact between the astrological factor and the electrifying essential planet energy which may sometimes even be a decisive influence in the life.

Placement of the Part in a house and its disposition show the focus of the part in a more psychological sense, for example Part of Fortune/Hunger in the ninth house gives a thirst for knowledge.

APPENDIX D

An Explanation of Dignities and Receptions

To be able to follow the case studies in this book you need to know the classical system of dignities. There are two kinds of dignities describing two kinds of power. The first dignity is called essential dignity, the second is accidental dignity (find more below). The degree of essential dignity is assessed by a planet's position in a sign. Mars in Aries is in its own sign and therefore has a lot of essential dignity. But Mars is also very strong in Capricorn where it has its exaltation and this is also essential dignity.

There are also negative counterparts of a placement of a planet in its own sign or in exaltation, and these are called 'detriment' and 'fall' respectively. In other words, when the planet is in the sign opposite to its rulership or exaltation. If a planet is placed in such a negative dignity, it cannot do much good and is 'essentially debilitated'. An example is Mars in Libra, opposite to its own sign, so in detriment. This is a difficult Mars which will cause trouble in some way. If Mars is placed in Cancer in opposition to its exaltation sign Capricorn, it also has no dignity (being in its 'fall') and will also work out in a negative way.

All planets have signs in which they are either very strong or very weak according to the logical pattern given below.

Sun strong: in its own sign Leo, exalted in Aries.
weak: in detriment in Aquarius opposite Leo and in fall in Libra opposite Aries.

Moon strong: in its own sign Cancer and exalted in Taurus.
weak: in detriment in Capricorn and in fall in Scorpio.

Mercury	strong: in its own signs Gemini and Virgo. weak: in detriment in Sagittarius, and in fall *and* detriment in Pisces. Virgo is Mercury's sign and the place of its exaltation, so it is extremely strong there.
Venus	strong: in its own signs Taurus and Libra, in exaltation in Pisces. weak: in detriment in Aries and Scorpio, in fall in Virgo.
Mars	strong: in its own signs Aries and Scorpio and exalted in Capricorn. weak in detriment in Libra and Taurus and in fall in Cancer.
Jupiter	strong in its own signs Sagittarius and Pisces and exalted in Cancer. weak: in detriment in Gemini and Virgo, in fall in Capricorn.
Saturn	strong in its own signs Aquarius and Capricorn and exalted in Libra. weak: in detriment in Leo and Cancer, in fall in Aries.

In this scheme only classical rulerships apply. Jupiter rules Pisces, Mars rules Scorpio and Saturn rules Aquarius. The outer planets have no role in this pattern, which is rigidly logical and easy to remember. Some astrologers do not use the term in detriment, they prefer 'in exile'. However detriment seems to describe better what this state means; the positive power a planet may have is absent, it is severely damaged. The normally positive planet Jupiter is quite nasty when it is in detriment.

Placement in its own sign, exaltation, detriment and fall are the most important dignities, describing the main differences in planetary power. There are three other smaller positive dignities, of which the elemental attributions are the most important. A planet placed in a sign of which the elemental nature accords well with its own nature has some power, although definitely not as much as a planet in own sign or in exaltation. If a planet is placed in the right element this is called 'in triplicity' in classical astrology. Triplicity is simply another word for element.

It is easy to check whether a planet is placed in its triplicity. The first step is to determine whether we have a day chart or a night chart. If the Sun is above the horizon in the houses 7 to 12 it is day chart. If it is under the horizon in the houses 1 to 6 it is a night chart. If this is clear we apply the following the scheme:

DAY CHARTS (DIURNAL)

Sun, Venus, Mars and Saturn may get extra essential dignity by placement in a fitting sign.

Essential dignity by triplicity: Sun in Fire signs, Saturn in Air signs, Mars in Water signs, Venus in Earth signs.

NIGHT CHARTS (NOCTURNAL)

Jupiter, the Moon, Mars and Mercury may get extra essential dignity by placement in a fitting sign.

Essential dignity by triplicity: Jupiter in Fire signs, Mercury in Air signs, Mars in Water signs, the Moon in Earth signs.

There is also another system giving each element three planets instead of two. Some classical astrologers claim that this system is better because it is older. In practice this point cannot be proven and the two-ruler system is as ancient as the three-ruler system. In all branches of astrology the two-ruler system is effective.

Besides triplicities there are also the minor dignities 'term' (*termini*: boundaries) and 'face' or decanate. These give a planet a small degree of extra power but not much. The terms are assessed on the basis of five planetary zones into which every sign can be divided, in each zone one planet is placed in its 'term'. Faces work in the same way but they divide the signs in three zones of ten degrees each. These minor dignities give much less power that the other dignities but they will sometimes be important. In the scheme below an overview of all the five essential dignities is given.

A Table of the Essential Dignities of the PLANETS according to Ptolemy

Sign	Houses of the Planets	Exalt-ation	Triplicity of Planets D	N	The Terms of the Planets					The Faces of the Planets			Detri ment	Fall
♈	♂ D	☉ 19	☉	♃	♃ 6	♀ 14	☿ 21	♂ 26	♄ 30	♂ 10	☉ 20	♀ 30	♀	♄
♉	♀ N	☽ 3	♀	☽	♀ 8	☿ 15	♃ 22	♄ 26	♂ 30	☿ 10	☽ 20	♄ 30	♂	
♊	☿ D	☊ 3	♄	☿	☿ 7	♃ 13	♀ 21	♄ 25	♂ 30	♃ 10	♂ 20	☉ 30	♃	
♋	☽ D/N	♃ 15	♂	♂	♂ 6	♃ 13	☿ 20	♀ 27	♄ 30	♀ 10	☿ 20	☽ 30	♄	♂
♌	☉ D/N		☉	♃	♄ 6	☿ 13	♀ 19	♃ 25	♂ 30	♄ 10	♃ 20	♂ 30	♄	
♍	☿ N	☿ 15	♀	☽	☿ 7	♀ 13	♃ 18	♄ 24	♂ 30	☉ 10	♀ 20	☿ 30	♃	♀
♎	♀ D	♄ 21	♄	☿	♄ 6	♀ 11	♃ 19	☿ 24	♂ 30	☽ 10	♄ 20	♃ 30	♂	☉
♏	♂ N		♂	♂	♂ 6	♃ 14	♀ 21	☿ 27	♄ 30	♂ 10	☉ 20	♀ 30	♀	☽
♐	♃ D	☋ 3	☉	♃	♃ 8	♀ 14	☿ 19	♄ 25	♂ 30	☿ 10	☽ 20	♄ 30	☿	
♑	♄ N	♂ 28	♀	☽	♀ 6	☿ 12	♃ 19	♂ 25	♄ 30	♃ 10	♂ 20	☉ 30	☽	♃
♒	♄ D		♄	☿	♄ 6	☿ 12	♀ 20	♃ 25	♂ 30	♀ 10	☿ 20	☽ 30	☉	
♓	♃ N	♀ 27	♂	♂	♀ 8	♃ 14	☿ 20	♂ 26	♄ 30	♄ 10	♃ 20	♂ 30	☿	☿

Table of Essential Dignities

Going from left to right, this table shows for each sign the planets 'having dignity' there. The first column next to the sign symbols gives the sign rulers, the second column the exaltation rulers and then the triplicity rulers are mentioned (first the ruler in a day chart, then the ruler in a night chart). Under 'terms' the term rulers are listed, five zones in each sign, and the last column the faces or decanate rulers having authority over zones of 10 degrees. The columns on the far right show the planets in detriment and fall through the signs. The specific degree numbers mentioned in the exaltation column indicate the place in the sign where the planet is extra-exalted. From the right to the left the rulers get weaker; the sign ruler is much more important than the ruler of a term or a face.

As an example, we can take Mercury in the ninth degree of Taurus in a diurnal chart. How much dignity does Mercury get there? The sign ruler of Taurus is Venus and the exaltation ruler is the Moon; this means that Taurus is a sign ruled by Venus and that the Moon is exalted there. Thus Venus and the Moon have lots of power there to work in a positive way. Mercury does not, and it will get no dignity through rulership or exaltation. The Lord of the earth triplicity is Venus in this diurnal chart, so Mercury does not get any essential dignity through triplicity either. But Mercury does have some dignity by term. The planet is placed in the second term of Taurus between 8 and 15 degrees and in this term Mercury rules so he is in the right place by term. The first decanate of Taurus, the first 10 degree zone of the sign, is also ruled by Mercury, so it also gets some strength through face. We then say that Mercury has term and face dignity. It's not much, but it is better than nothing at all and much better than debilitation by fall or detriment.

Another term to be explained is 'peregrine'. A planet is peregrine when it has no dignity at all, positive or negative. It is not placed in its own sign or in exaltation, triplicity, term, face, detriment or fall. Peregrine means drifting; it is not bad, it is not good, it just has no direction. That is why it tends to be challenging - because things that have no clear direction can go astray quite easily. It is often said that a planet is in detriment or fall **and** peregrine because it has no positive dignity. This is wrong; a planet in a bad state is downright bad, a drifting planet drifts and this is not the same thing. It cannot be neutral and bad at the same time.

We also need to consider the benefics and malefics. The benefics are Jupiter and Venus and these planets tend to have an effect which is pleasant for us. But this is only true if they have some essential dignity; their benefic nature is diminished as they lose dignity. Jupiter in detriment in Virgo for example cannot be called benefic any more, it is an 'accidental' malefic and it will not work out well. Saturn and Mars are malefics by nature and tend to have unpleasant effects. However, if the malefics have essential dignity, they lose much of their malefic character and may even work out better than expected. The other three planets are more or less neutral although the same dignity principle applies; the more essential dignity they have the more positive their effects are.

Accidental dignity

The degree of essential dignity or planetary power shows its quality, how purely and effectively it can function. Venus in Libra is totally Venus and in this condition the planet can act according to its nature. The other kind of dignity is called accidental and it shows the force with which a planet can manifest in the world. The point is not whether this planet is working as it was meant according to its nature, it only shows how strong its influence in the world is. Accidental dignity measures quantity, essential dignity measures quality. We can use the simple scheme below to assess the degree of accidental dignity.

> **Strong**: placement in an angular house, in the 11th house, fast movement (not for Saturn), direct movement, no narrow aspects with malefics, joy (see below), conjunction with the favorable fixed stars *Spica* and *Regulus*.
>
> **Moderate**: placement in houses 2, 3, 5 or 9
>
> **Weak**: conjunction or opposition with the Sun (combust), retrograding, placement in the malefic houses 6, 8 or 12, very slow movement (not for Saturn), narrow aspects with malefics, besiegement (placement between aspects with two malefics), in opposition with the house it joys in, on the malefic fixed star *Algol*.

The Moon is weak when waning and strong when waxing. In the *via combusta*, the 'burnt road' from 15 Libra to 15 Scorpio, the Moon is weakened too. The North Node expands and strengthens and a conjunction with the North Node is generally positive, however when something like the cause of an illness is conjunct this expansive force it is not favourable. The South Node will diminish things and inhibit, and is mostly negative.

Joy is an accidental dignity derived from placement in a 'good' house, a house where the planet feels at home by nature: Mercury in the first house, the Moon in the third house, Venus in the fifth house, Mars in the sixth house, the Sun in the ninth house, Jupiter in the eleventh house and Saturn in the twelfth house. A planet in its joy feels okay and therefore has some more force to manifest itself in the world. A planet in opposition with its house of joy does not feel okay and so is weakened.

A very damaging debilitation is combustion, a conjunction with the Sun. When the orb between a planet and the Sun in conjunction is less than 8.30 degrees this is called combustion, which harms the planet and affects its ability to do much. Between 8.30 and 17.30 degrees from the Sun it is termed 'under the Sun's beams'. This is also difficult but not anything like as bad as combustion. There is a special case: a planet precisely conjunct the Sun is called cazimi and this is extremely powerful - a cazimi planet cannot be stopped. The orb for cazimi is 17.30 minutes of arc so we do not see this too often.

There are also the accidental dignities of hayz and halb, referring to the correct position a planet has in a chart that makes it stronger. Halb means in the correct half of the chart. The diurnal planets Saturn, Sun and Jupiter should be above the horizon in diurnal charts and below the horizon in nocturnal charts, and vice versa for the nocturnal planets Moon, Venus and Mars. To be in hayz, which means making the planet accidentally stronger than if it is only halb, the diurnal masculine planets have to placed not only in the correct part of the chart but also in a masculine sign. The nocturnal feminine planets Venus and the Moon should be in halb and in feminine signs to be in hayz. (Air-Fire signs are masculine, Earth-Water signs feminine). Mars is masculine and nocturnal, a Mercury rising before the Sun is diurnal otherwise nocturnal. Hayz/halb is only one of many accidental dignities and its importance should not be exaggerated.

Saturn, Jupiter and Mars will be accidentally stronger if they rise before the Sun (oriental position), while the Moon, Venus and Mercury are stronger rising after the Sun (occidental position), and they become weaker by being in the reversed positions. Gaining in north latitude (that is with increasing visibility in the sky) will make a planet stronger; increasing south latitude weaker. This is all very understandable, as accidental dignity has to with the power to manifest in the world.

Receptions

Receptions are of crucial importance in astrology; they show how the planets affect each other and whether they harm or help each other. To assess these connections we need the table of essential dignities. An example will show how this works. Suppose we are assessing the effects of Mercury in Aries in the life. The most important receptions Mercury makes from Aries will guide the analysis of the chart further. The general rule in analysing receptions is that a planet in a sign will have a positive effect on its dispositors and a negative effect on the planets in fall and detriment in this sign. So Mercury in Aries has a negative influence on Venus (which has its detriment in Aries) and Saturn (which has its fall in Aries). It works positively on Mars (sign ruler of Aries) and the Sun (which has its exaltation in Aries). Receptions also work through the weaker triplicity, term and face dispositors, but these receptions will obviously be weaker.

Through the network of receptions we can map all these connections between the relevant significators systematically, and we should always carry out such an analysis before proceeding further.

Epilogue

And when he had opened the seventh seal, there was silence in heaven about the space of half an hour. And I saw the seven angels which stood before God; and to them were given seven trumpets.

The Apocalypse of Saint John 8:1-6

Bibliography

Unfortunately there are no books about the lunar mansions in Western astrology which offer a complete and consistent logical method with worked examples. They just don't exist as far as I could gather. There is only information scattered in several texts, some of which have been mentioned below.

Al Biruni, *Elements of the Art of Astrology* (1029), Ascella, London, England, facsimile 1934.

Titus Burckhardt, *Mystical Astrology according to Ibn 'Arabi,* Fons Vitae, Louisville, US, 2001.

Sacred Art in East and West, Fons Vitae, Louisville, US, 2001.

John Frawley, *The Horary Textbook,* Apprentice Books, London, England, 2005.

The Real Astrology, Apprentice Books, London, England, 2000.

The Real Astrology Applied, Apprentice Books, London, England, 2002.

René Guénon, *The Esoterism of Dante,* Sophia Perennis, Hillsdale, US, 2001.

The Great Triad, Sophia Perennis, Hillsdale, US, 2001

The King of the World, Sophia Perennis, Hillsdale, US, 2001.

The Reign of Quantity and the Signs of the Times, Sophia Perennis, Hillsdale, US , 2001

Spiritual Authority & Temporal Power, Sophia Perennis, Hillsdale, US, 2001.

The Symbolism of the Cross, Sophia Perennis, Hillsdale, US, 2001.

Symbols of Sacred Science, Sophia Perennis, Hillsdale, US , 2004.

Traditional Forms and Cosmic Cycles, Sophia Perennis, Hillsdale, US, 2001.

Oscar Hofman, *Fixed Stars in the Chart: Constellations, Mansions and Mythology,* The Wessex Astrologer, Swanage, England, 2019.

Classical Medical Astrology – Healing with the Elements, The Wessex Astrologer, Swanage, England, 2009.

William Lilly, *Christian Astrology, Book 3* (1647), Ascella, London England, 2001.

Bibliography

Marcus Manilius, *Astronomica, Book 5* (Second Century).

Henry Cornelius Agrippa of Nettesheim -*Three Books of Occult Philosophy (translation Donald Tyson)*, Llewellyn Publications, St Paul US, 1997.

Ptolemaeus, *Tetrabiblos* (tweede eeuw), The Astrology Centre of America, Bel Air, US 2002.

Vivian Robson, *The Fixed Stars and Constellations in Astrology* (1923), Ascella, London, England, 2001.

Frithjof Schuon, *The Transcendent Unity of Religion,* Quest Books, Seattle, US, 1993.

Christopher Warnock, T*he Mansions of the Moon, A Lunar Zodiac for Astrology and Magic*, Renaissance Astrology, Iowa, US, 2010

About the author

Oscar Hofman lives in Gorinchem, The Netherlands, and practises all branches of traditional astrology: medical, natal, electional, horary and mundane. He is the founder of the International School of Classical Astrology offering a full training program in the tradition (horary, electional/natal, medical and mundane) in six languages, followed by students worldwide in more than 30 countries. He travels widely to teach and has clients in many nations around the world. He has written five books on horary practice, medical astrology, fixed stars and lunar mansions, published in six languages. He was the first European astrologer to be translated into Chinese.

He is also seen as one of the world's leading experts in classical medical astrology and in November 2007 his book on traditional medical astrology – the first publication in this field since 1677 - appeared in The Netherlands. It has been translated into Russian, French, English, Greek, Chinese and German.

He can be reached through oshofman@xs4all.nl, website (with international agenda): www.pegasus-advies.com or by phone 00-31-183-649405. On his website he writes a weekly blog in English.

www.ingramcontent.com/pod-product-compliance
Lightning Source LLC
Chambersburg PA
CBHW050800160426
43192CB00010B/1582